D0753725

Advanced Object-Oriented Analysis and Design Using UML

SIGS REFERENCE LIBRARY

Donald G. Firesmith
Editor-in-Chief

Additional Volumes in Preparation

NATIONAL UNIVERSITY
LIBRARY   SAN DIEGO

Advanced Object-Oriented Analysis and Design Using UML

James J. Odell

NATIONAL UNIVERSITY
SAN DIEGO LIBRARY

COPUBLISHED BY THE PRESS SYNDICATE OF THE UNIVERSITY OF CAMBRIDGE
AND SIGS BOOKS
The Pitt Building, Trumpington Street, Cambridge CB2 1RP, United Kingdom

CAMBRIDGE UNIVERSITY PRESS
The Edinburgh Building, Cambridge CB2 2RU, UK   http://www.cup.cam.ac.uk
40 West 20th Street, New York, NY 10011-4211, USA   http://www.cup.org
10 Stamford Road, Oakleigh, Melbourne 3166, Australia

SIGS Books & Multimedia   http://www.sigs.com
71 West 23rd Street, Third floor
New York, NY 10010

© 1998 by SIGS Books & Multimedia.

All rights reserved.

This book is in copyright. Subject to statutory exception
and to the provisions of relevant collective licensing agreements,
no reproduction of any part may take place without
the written permission of Cambridge University Press.

Any product mentioned in this book may be a trademark of its company.

First published in 1998

Printed in the United States of America

Design and composition by Barbara Crawford
Cover design by Brian Griesbaum

Typeset in Callisto and Optima

A catalog record for this book is available from the British Library

Library of Congress Cataloging-in-Publication Data is available.

ISBN 0-521-64819-X paperback

About the Author

James Odell is a consultant, writer, and educator in the areas of object orientation (OO), enterprise resource planning, and business reengineering. Throughout most of his thirty-year career, Mr. Odell has been heavily involved in developing better methods to understand, communicate, and manage system requirements. He was one of the early innovators of information engineering methodologies. Formerly, he was the principal consultant for KnowledgeWare, Inc., where he pioneered and taught the concepts of data modeling, information strategy planning, and CASE technology application. Now, he is one of the first practical implementors of object-oriented analysis and design. Working with the OMG and other major methodologists, he continues to innovate and improve OO methods and techniques. In particular, he participated in the development of the CORBA/UML and was the cochair of the OMG's Object Analysis and Design Task Force. Mr. Odell conducts international seminars and workshops and provides consulting to major companies worldwide.

He has recently coauthored books with James Martin entitled *Object-Oriented Analysis and Design* (1992; Prentice Hall), *Object-Oriented Methods: A Foundation* (1995; Prentice Hall), and *Object-Oriented Methods: Pragmatic Considerations* (1996; Prentice Hall). Additionally, he is a columnist for the *Journal of Object-Oriented Programming* (JOOP) and *Distributed Object Computing* (DOC). He can be contacted at jodell@compuserve.com.

Foreword

One of the biggest risks in software development is writing the wrong software. You spend time with cool technological tools—OO programming languages, distributed systems, persistence frameworks, impressive GUI technology—and yet still fail because the software you build does not actually help the user do the job they want to do. Unless you understand what your users do—the tasks they engage in, the business they are in—you cannot build a system that will work for them. However good your technology, the *essential* problem in software development is that of understanding what system you should be building.

Jim Odell learned this lesson developing database systems long before the object craze had made any impact outside PARC. In the 80's he was a leading developer of Information Engineering, but he left that world just as it became popular because he felt objects were a better way of linking the software with the way business works.

But his view of objects was always that of a conceptual slant, always thinking about how people should think about the world rather than the limitations of existing (and ever changing) technology. Such ideas as dynamic and multiple classification, power types, and business rules are a result of this seeking of ways to better express peoples' mental models—models that act as a solid foundation for design.

Many people think of this analysis modeling as a high level, fuzzy, waffly exercise. Jim has always thought otherwise. Without a precise idea of how your concepts work, how can you build instructions for an unforgiving computer? So throughout his work is a strong sense of rigor, of thinking hard about the meaning behind notations.

The essays on Aggregation are a fine example of this. Aggregation is usually treated as little more than decorative modeling and is usually devoid of any real semantics. By thinking further into the depths of what we conceptually mean by aggregation, he gives a notoriously fluffy part of modeling the foundations on which something truly useful can be said.

Many pundits like to put forward all ideas as though they were their ideas alone. Over the years, Jim has frequently worked with other lesser-known practitioners and has encouraged them to share the limelight with him. As one of those partners, I can attest to the fact that Jim is no passive partner but a skillful craftsman of both ideas and the way to express them. Like many others, I've always enjoyed working and writing with Jim, and that is reflected in the quality of people who have shared his column over the years.

In the last couple of years, much of Jim's life has been dominated by the drive to standardize an object modeling language. Jim has always seen the method wars as an unnecessary irritant, something that gets in the way of both users and creative methodologists, so he has spent a lot of time and money working in OMG to get methodologists to agree to a common modeling language. It is appropriate, therefore, to see these articles updated to use the resulting Unified Modeling Language (UML). These give us all a chance to see how Jim's conceptual slant fits in with this new standard, which makes this book appealing even to those of us who already have Jim's previous articles and books.

Jim's ideas have been a big influence on my thinking and practice. I think you will find here some valuable thoughts that will help you use object modeling to its full potential.

MARTIN FOWLER

Preface

In 1974, I became convinced that system developers should model the system before building it. I learned that the more I understood the system requirements, the better the system fit the organization's needs. (I don't mean just writing a lot of prose and calling them "specifications.") I found that by also using graphical representations of various system aspects, I could improve understanding and communication between (and among) users and developers. Since I built my first CASE tool in 1976, I have been trying to refine both the content and process of business modeling.

This book contains some of my latest thoughts. Originally, the chapters were developed as articles in SIGS publications. However, two things have changed since their original publication. First, I have had time to exercise my ideas more and improve them. Second, a common notation has been developed and approved by the OMG called UML. This de facto notation standard includes most of the notions that were important to me prior to the standard—including event diagrams, power types, and constraints. Many of the actual names and symbols differ from those used in Information Engineering for over 15 years. However, I am content to change them if it means that the "religious notation wars" are over and more of us can communicate easier and more accurately. This book, then, contains a set of articles—improved and standardized.

The term "advanced" is used in the title because I am trying to push the envelope called object orientation. Traditionally, OO does not include such notions as multilevel meta-modeling, structural constraints, power types, and business rules. However, these notions are not only useful, but they can be defined on top of the foundation we know as object orientation. (When OO gets enough of these extensions, perhaps a whole new approach may be born.)

UML includes a recommended meta-model and notation for various kinds of diagrams. There are three areas where this book might appear to differ from UML. First, I use verbs rather than nouns as role names in class diagrams. This is not a departure from the standard, because neither verbs nor nouns are explicitly addressed by UML. And, since most of the modeling approaches until now have used verbs, I use them here to cushion the culture shock. (There are many who are still adamant in their position that verbs communicate roles better than nouns do.) Second, for the sake of clarity this book will use full, rather than abbreviated, cardinality constraints (multiplicity). Finally, the term *object type* will be used instead of *type*. Currently, UML has a notion called *class*, which can be stereotyped as both *type* and *implementation class*. Again, to reduce the amount of change brought on by UML, this book will use the term *object type* to mean *type*. Since the OMG still uses both terms virtually synonymously, I don't feel that this usage will cause major confusion—and I hope that the UML purists will be able to handle my decision.

Acknowledgments

Several articles in this book were coauthored. I feel that people working together make improvement and evolution possible. In the case of the following chapters, I would like to express my gratitude for the following coauthors: Martin Fowler, Conrad Bock, and Guus Ramackers. In addition, people at IntelliCorp, James Martin and Co., and Quoin helped to refine and bring alive many of the concepts in this book. Finally, I would like to express particular appreciation to Andrea Matthies, who transformed the text of this book.

Contents

Part I
Structural Issues

In OO analysis, the developer learns to draw diagrams that express the types and relationships required for a given system. For the average developer, this is exactly what is required—or is it? What about those developers who are creating or using repositories and data warehouses. Are simple types and relationships enough? And finally, what about those developers who want to have the same or a greater degree of formalism than is found in relational databases? If relational databases have a relational algebra, why can't OO languages and databases have an "object algebra"?

This section pushes beyond the traditional "boxes and lines" to a deeper and more encompassing understanding. *Modeling Objects Using Binary vs Entity-Relationship Approaches* challenges the developer's beliefs about which modeling approach is the "correct" way. There are three basic approaches to representing structural modeling. The modeler must choose the approach that provides the best clarity on a situation-by-situation basis—not on a good or bad basis.

Object Types as Objects and Vice Versa discusses modeling meta-levels and why they are important. *Power Types* extends meta-level concepts to a explain a new and important concept that all developers should be incorporating in their everyday modeling activity.

Often, "boxes and lines" are not enough to express certain system requirements. *Specifying Structural Constraints* adds to the modeler's toolbox by providing ways to express restrictions to the ways objects may be related. Such constraints are not available in traditional notations.

The last article in this section proposes a way to formalize OO notions used in analysis. Such a formalization provides the basis for an "object algebra" such as the Object Constraint Language in UML. *Toward A Formalization for OO Analysis* proceeds from first principles and develops a recommended ontology for thinking about and expressing the fundamental concepts of OO analysis.

Modeling Objects: Using Binary- and Entity-Relationship Approaches

June 1992

The International Organization for Standardization (ISO) has identified three groups of approaches for conceptually modeling the structural aspects of systems: binary-relationship models, entity-attribute-relationship models, and interpreted predicate logic [Griethuysen, 1987]. Binary-relationship (BR) models basically represent types related to other types. While these models are called *binary,* many practitioners also use the approach to express n-ary associations. Entity-attribute-relationship (EAR) models are similar to BR models, except that EAR models also incorporate a notion of attribute type that is separate from relationship type. Interpreted predicate logic (IPL) is expressed as sentences encoded in some formal language. For example, the following IPL statement asserts that a car is of one and only one model:

Models = { $\underline{m}$ | $\underline{m}$ is a model }
Cars $\subset \cup$ Models
$\forall \underline{m} \forall \underline{m}'$
 (If $\underline{m} \in$ Models & $\underline{m}' \in$ Models & $\neg (\underline{m} = \underline{m}') \rightarrow \underline{m} \cap \underline{m}' = \emptyset$)

While IPL expressions are exacting, they are not very user friendly and require extensive training. However, the approaches of both binary-relationship modeling and entity-attribute-relationship modeling are reasonably easy to understand with little training. In this column, I will discuss how these two groups of approaches can be applied in an OO context.

BR VERSUS EAR MODELS

Binary-Relationship Models

Binary-relationship models have their roots in artificial intelligence and linguistics. Basically, they express types of things and associations between these types. For example, Fig. 1.1 depicts such types as Car, Color, and Day and various associations between these types.

On the surface, Fig. 1.1 resembles an entity-attribute-relationship diagram. However, the major difference between BR models and EAR models is the way in which associations are represented. EAR models represent associations in a way that they appear both *within* and *outside* of a type. BR models have no notion of associations appearing within a type. So, just how important is this distinction to OO?

In object orientation, an *attribute* is defined as an identifiable association from a given object to some other object or set of objects [Soley, 1992]. An *attribute type,* then, is an identifiable association from one *type* of object to another *type* of object.* For example, in Fig. 1.1 home-office location is an attribute type of Manufacturer. Manufacturer is a type of object and Location is another. The association from each Manufacturer object to a Location object is— by definition—an attribute of the Manufacturer object. The *inverse* of the home-office location attribute type is an attribute type of Location called manufacturers. Here, each Location object has an attribute that associates with zero or more Manufacturer objects.†

For those who prefer using verb phrases instead of nouns, the home-office location attribute type could be named has home-office at. Both are valid names for the same attribute type. The choice of whether to use verbs or nouns is a personal one and will be discussed in the last section.

Entity-Attribute-Relationship Models

As defined above, an OO *attribute type* is an identifiable association from one *type* of object to another *type* of object. For EAR models, such associations appear diagrammatically either *within* or *outside* of entity types. Those that appear *within* an entity type are called *attribute types* (henceforth called *EAR attribute types* to avoid further confusion). Those associations *outside*

---

* Multi-argumented attribute types, which map from more than one object, will not be discussed here.

† In other words, the inverse associates each Location object with those Manufacturer objects whose home office *is* that Location object.

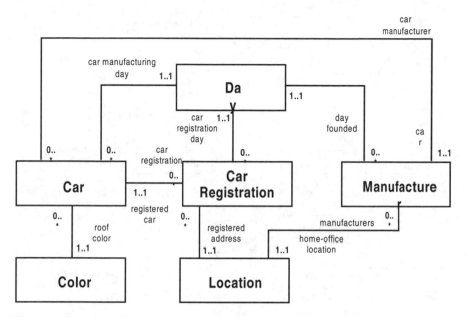

Figure 1.1.   An object schema representing a car-related example.

of an entity type are represented in terms of *relationship types* with other entity types. Technically, the object types and associations in a BR model can be expressed in an EAR model with a combination of EAR attribute types and relationship types [Chen, 1981].

Figure 1.2(a) depicts one way of diagramming the BR model in Fig. 1.1. This EAR diagram employs a mixture of EAR attribute types and relationship types. For instance, car manufacturer and car registration appear on two different relationship types. They are those portions that map from the Car entity type to the Car Manufacturer and Car Registration entity types—as they are in the BR model. In contrast, car manufacturing day and roof color have become EAR attribute types *within* the Car entity type.

In addition to Fig. 1.2(a), the diagram in Fig. 1.1 could also be read as an EAR diagram. However, the EAR diagrams have no EAR attribute types, only relationship types. Another extreme is illustrated in Fig. 1.2(b), which represents all of the BR model associations solely as EAR attribute types. With Fig. 1.1 and Fig. 1.2(b) being two very unlikely extremes, Fig. 1.2(a) is just one of the acceptable solutions in the middle. The actual solution selected is determined by the EAR analyst and the user expert in an analysis session. One commonly adopted guideline is that EAR attributes map objects to literals or to a collection of literals while relationships do not.

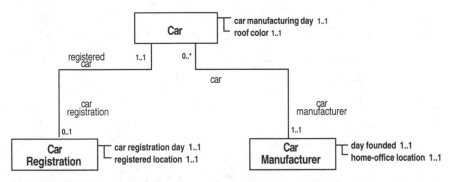

(a) EAR model example with both EAR attribute types and relationship types.

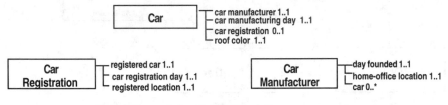

(b) EAR model with EAR attribute types only.

Figure 1.2.   Two possible EAR mapping solutions for the BR model in Fig. 1.1.

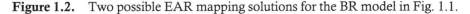

(For example, the age attibute of a particular Person could be "42" or the height could be "72". In the car example, a given car's roof color could be the literal "chartreuse" and the car manufacturing day "01/04/92".)

An Important Difference Between EAR and BR Models

At first glance, the only difference between the EAR and BR approaches is that EAR models have EAR attribute types and BR do not. However, another big difference exists. The EAR models depicted in Fig. 1.2 indicate fewer object types than the corresponding BR model in Fig. 1.1. Is this important? Will it matter in an OO environment if object types, such as Day or Color, are not explicitly specified? The ramifications of this difference are discussed in the next section.

THE RAMIFICATIONS OF OBJECT TYPES FOR OO DESIGN

In object-oriented programming languages (OOPLs), object types can be implemented as classes. Each class determines a set of objects. In addition, each class defines the data structure of its objects and the operations that are permitted on them.

Classes Determine Sets of Objects

Figure 1.3 is an example that illustrates the associations between two types of objects: Car and Day. As expressed in Fig. 1.1, the car manufacturing day BR attribute type defines a mapping from each Car object to exactly one Day object. This same specification could be implemented in an OOPL as Car and Day classes, where each Car object could have a pointer to a Day object. The set of all Car objects are those manufactured on a specific day. The Day set would comprise only those objects that are valid days. For instance, the Day object named June 30, 1991, would be a member of this set, June 31, 1991, would not. Moreover, the car manufacturing day function ensures that a given Car maps to a valid Day. When implemented in this way, the Day set acts like a calendar to which other objects can relate.

The Day object type does not have to be implemented as a Day class. A table of valid days—or a mechanism to compute them—could be placed in those classes relating to the notion of Day. Instead of organizing Day

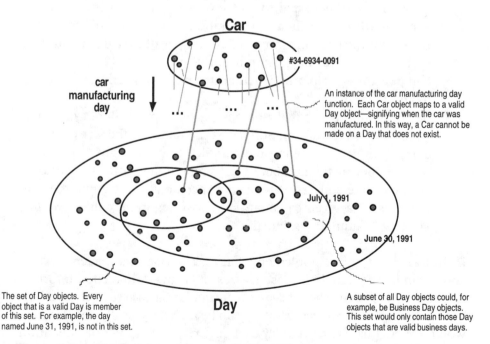

An instance of the car manufacturing day function. Each Car object maps to a valid Day object—signifying when the car was manufactured. In this way, a Car cannot be made on a Day that does not exist.

The set of Day objects. Every object that is a valid Day is member of this set. For example, the day named June 31, 1991, is not in this set.

A subset of all Day objects could, for example, be Business Day objects. This set would only contain those Day objects that are valid business days.

Figure 1.3.   The Day set consists of all the valid dates.

information via a single class, it could be redundantly specified within those classes that require it. For instance, the Car and Manufacturer classes could define their own date-processing routines and tables, instead of interfacing with a Day class. The choice belongs to the OO designer and is based on performance and space considerations. To properly assist the OO designer in making correct implementation decisions, the OO analyst must clearly specify *all* object types. Those object types not clearly specified by the OO analysis can hardly be implemented correctly in the final system. If the Day object type in the example above is *not* specified during analysis, the designer may not implement its functionality in a useful and efficient way.

Classes Organize Structure and Operation

As mentioned earlier, each class defines the structure of its objects along with the operations permitted on each of its objects. For instance, the Day class would define the structure of each Day object along with the various operations that access and maintain this structure. In this way, the Day operations could include such operations as

- validation—validating a given day to be correct. For example, if the Day class were requested to create or associate to a Day object for June 31, 1991, the validation operation would reject the request.
- incrementing/decrementing—increasing or decreasing a date by a specific number of days, months, or years.
- comparison—comparing whether one day is earlier, later, or equal to another.
- determination of weekday names—given a particular Day, such as June 30, 1991, returning Sunday as the name of the weekday.
- computation of shopping days until Christmas—given a specific day, computing the number of days remaining until Christmas.
- calendar date conversion—given a specific day, returning the date in terms of a given calendar, such as Gregorian, Julian, Arabic, Hebrew, Hindu, and sidereal.

If the Day object type is implemented as a class, operations such as those above can be requested by those classes requiring date-related information. For instance, the day founded of a particular Car Manufacturer must be a bona fide date before the association can be made. Typically, the Day class would ensure this. Without a Day class, the responsibility for a validation of this kind resides with the Car Manufacturer class. If the only time such validations occur are with Car Manufacturers, this presents no problems. However, if any other class requires the same Day operations, they must either reference the code in the Car Manufacturer class or write redundant code. Referencing code in an existing module is the goal of good modular programming. However, the programmer must know which module contains the code and where it is located. In very small systems, this is easy. In highly automated companies, it is virtually impossible—unless an OO approach is adopted. In OOPLs, each operation is associated with the class of objects on which it operates. Validating a date would be associated with the Day class, creating or destroying a Car with the Car class, and so on. In short, the class acts as an index for both structure and operation in the OO world.

How does all this relate back to EAR models that specify fewer object types than corresponding BR models?

ENSURING EAR MODELS SUPPORT OO DESIGN

The entity-relationship models in Fig. 1.2 neither contain nor indicate the need for a Day entity type. Yet in actuality, three of the entity types have attribute types that are Day-related. Since the specification does not explicitly make this fact clear, the OO designer (or code generator) has no way of knowing that a Day class should even be considered as a useful OOPL implementation.

Does this mean that analysts can no longer use EAR attribute types if they wish to produce object-oriented designs? Some analysts find that making the distinction between EAR attribute types and relationship types is highly useful. On the other hand, some analysts prefer the BR model approach which does not make the distinction. Can both approaches be accommodated in an OO environment?

A Solution

Every OO attribute type maps to an object type. Therefore, *every* EAR attribute type and relationship type maps to an entity type. For example in Fig. 1.2(a), registered car defines a mapping from the Car Registration entity type to the Car entity type. Car Registration also defines an EAR attribute type named car registration day. However, this association does *not* specify the entity type to which it maps. Without this specification, the notion of Day cannot be explicitly communicated to the OO designer. In Fig. 1.2(a), this same omission also applies to those attribute types related to color and location. Without explicitly specifying the entity types to which these attribute types map, Color and Location could easily be overlooked as possible classes.

The good news is that many advanced EAR practitioners already specify the type to which an EAR attribute type maps. Some practitioners refer to this notion as a *class word, value set,* or *domain.* In IBM's AD Cycle, it is called the *information type.* Figure 1.4(a) illustrates how Fig. 1.2(a) might be more completely expressed so that *all* types are identified. When specified in this way, the types specified in attributes are types in their own right. If the analyst wishes, these same types can also be represented as entity types, as depicted in Fig. 1.4(b).

In addition to the type, the inverse cardinality constraint is also required. For example, while a Car must have exactly one Color via roof color, inversely that same Color can be associated with zero or more Cars. The notation following the types in Fig. 1.4(a) indicates the inverse cardinality constraint as specified in Fig. 1.1. With this extra notation, the EAR and BR models can express equivalent meaning, though the inverse is not always implemented (particularly in the association from Color to Car). However, implementation is not the issue in OO analysis. The primary goal of analysis is to model the end-user's concepts and leave the concept implementation to the designers.

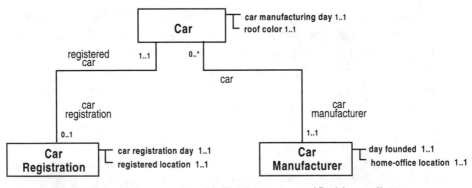

(a) EAR model example with EAR types specified in attributes.

(b) EAR information types from Fig. 1.6a expressed as entity types.

Figure 1.4.   EAR types in attributes identified and represented as entity types.

ONE LAST ISSUE: NAMING ATTRIBUTES

So far in this column, nouns have been used to name OO attribute types. Some developers find this useful because they prefer nouns for field names in programs. Since fields can be specified on the basis of OO attribute types, employing the same name for both is convenient. For example, the Car Registration attribute types defined in Fig. 1.1 could map to a class in the following way:

```
class
    Car Registration
        registered car : Car;
        car registration day : Day;
        registered location : Location;
```

In EAR models, nouns are conventionally used to label EAR attribute types. However, most modelers label EAR relationship types with verb names.* For those modelers preferring verbs, a modified version of the BR model in Fig. 1.1 is depicted in Fig. 1.5(a). These Car Registration attribute types could map to a class in the following way:

```
class
    Car Registration
        registers : Car;
        registered on : Day;
        registered for : Location;
```

Figure 1.5(b) illustrates one possible mapping of the BR model to an EAR model. Notice that the EAR attribute names are verbs, not nouns. If nouns are used as names on a BR diagram, the names on the EAR relationship types will not be verbs. Therefore, using only verbs or only nouns to name BR attribute types produces nonstandard results when mapping to EAR diagrams. Basically, the analyst has two choices:

1. Define both a verb and a noun form for each OO attribute type, so that when the association is mapped to an EAR model, the standard naming form can be chosen.

---

* Nouns were used initially to label EAR relationship types as well [Chen, 1976].

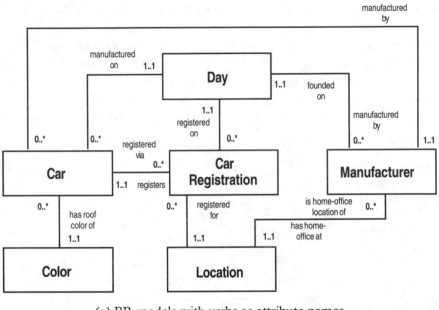

(a) BR models with verbs as attribute names.

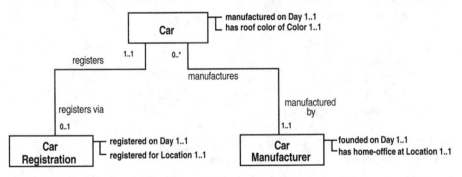

(b) An EAR diagram mapping from the BR model above.

Figure 1.5.   Verb names on OO attribute types map to verbs on both EAR attribute and relationship types.

2. Use only nouns or only verbs on OO attribute types and accept that EAR attribute types and relationship types will have the same naming convention.

Personally, I prefer using only noun names for OO attribute types. Some people don't care. Some demand an almost religious adherence to verbs on relationship types and nouns on EAR attribute types. The point is: choose what is the most useful and communicates most clearly.

SUMMARY

This column discusses some of the differences between binary-relationship and entity-relationship models and how these two approaches can be applied in an OO context. The major difference between BR models and EAR models is that EAR models can express OO attribute types that are "within" an entity type. Object schemas have no such notion.

The OO attribute type is a mapping of objects from one type to another. However, object-oriented design problems can result if the EAR attribute type is not properly specified in this manner. To avoid these problems

- identify *every* EAR attribute type with its information type and inverse cardinality constraint, and
- define the information type is an object type in its own right.

REFERENCES

Chen, Peter Pin-Shan, "The Entity-Relationship Model-Toward a Unified View of Data," *ACM Transactions on Database Systems,* 1:1, March 1976, pp. 9–36.

Chen, Peter Pin-Shan, "A Preliminary Framework for Entity-Relationship Models," *Entity-Relationship Approach to Information Modeling and Analysis,* Proceedings of the 2nd International Conference on Entity-Relationship Approach (Washington, DC), Peter Pin-Shan Chen ed., ER Institute, New Orleans, pp. 19–23.

Griethuysen, J. J. van, ed., *Information Processing Systems—Concepts and Terminology for the Conceptual Schema and the Information Base,* International Organization for Standardization, Technical ISO/TR 9007: 1987(E), March 15, 1982 (revised July 1, 1987).

Soley, Richard Mark, ed., *Object Management Architecture Guide,* Object Management Group, Document 92.11.1, September 1, 1992.

Object Types as Objects and Vice Versa

February 1992

The fact that *types* of objects are objects in their own right is a mathematically fundamental notion of object orientation. Without it, we would not be able to produce meta-models. However, most OO environments do not support this notion very well. Yet, the notion is vital for many applications of OO technology—particularly when producing meta-models or data warehouses.

META-MODELING

The conventional approach to meta-modeling involves three levels. A *meta-model* is a model that defines other models.

> A *meta-model* is a model of models. It contains object types whose instances are also object types.

For example, a meta-model could define instances of object types, such as Object Type, Relationship Type, Attribute Type, and Operation. These object types would then dictate the way in which the next level would be expressed. For example, a meta-model with an object type called Operation would allow the *model* level to instantiate types of processes such as Assemble Part or Pay Employee. The meta-model object type called Object Type would instantiate *model*-level occurrences such as Person or Product.

Continuing down, the *model*-level object types determine the types of *data* and *process* instances that can occur in an enterprise. For example, Pay Employee at the model level instantiates all the various processing moments when an enterprise pays its employees. An Employee object type at the model level instantiates all the instances of enterprise employees.

These three levels,* indicated in Fig. 2.1, might seem to reflect a natural division in model building. However, if each level is supposed to define the basis for instantiating the next, three levels are not enough. For example, the model level contains several instances of Object Type. The Object Type named Product Type applies to several instances at the data and process level, such as "Sony CD Player" and "B&O Turntable." As far as the salesperson at a hi-fi store is concerned, these are most certainly two instances of the products offered.

However, for the inventory clerk in the hi-fi store, the "Sony CD Player" is a *type* of product for sale, and the important objects are really *instances* of Sony CD Player. The bottom line, then, is that the inventory clerk is interested in the instances of the instances of Product Type. For example, if Sony CD Player is an instance of Product Type, the clerk may have two instances of a Sony CD Player identified by the serial numbers "V4572870" and "V4572871." In other words, the salesperson's object is the clerk's object type. Instances of the clerk's object type are a level "below" the data and process level.

Maintaining Modeling Levels in CASE Tools

Most CASE tools maintain models and meta-models as physically separate levels (Fig. 2.2). In order to change the kinds of object types that can be defined at the model level, a meta-model must be modified. For example, if an organization decides to support the "function decomposition" of activities, the meta-model must be changed to allow an Operation tree structure. While this separation of model and meta-model seems sensible, the rigid physical separation present in most CASE tools can be troublesome for several reasons.

First, the rigid physical separation in a CASE tool usually means that the model level cannot reference instances in the meta-model level. For example, the diagram in Fig. 2.3 expresses that each Measurement is associated with an Object it measures. Measurement resides at the model level; Object, however,

---

* Since the metal-model level in turn has a meta-level, this additional level is sometimes referred to as the *meta-meta*-level.

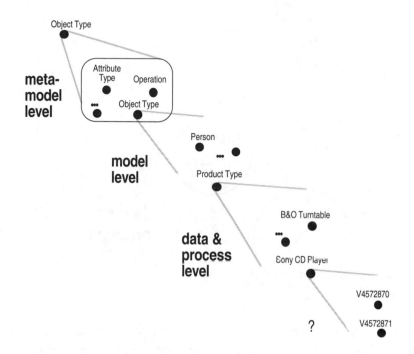

Figure 2.1.   Meta-modeling defines those types of objects whose instances are also types of objects.

is at a higher meta-level than Measurement. As such, this cannot be supported by most CASE tools. (Technically, Object can be specified at the model level. However, most CASE tools will consider a model-level instance named Object to be different than a meta-level instance with the same name.)

Second, modifying separately maintained meta-models is often impossible. The software vendor may provide no customization features or may implicitly define the meta-model in the form of program code. In addition, the software vendor may consider the contents of its meta-model to be proprietary.

Third, rigid three-level modeling falters when some data and process level structure also has instances (such as the B&O Turntable and Sony CD Player illustrated in Fig. 2.1). Should yet-another modeling level be added to accommodate these instances? If the ability to instantiate at the model level were allowed, any number of levels could be defined within it. This ability could be supported by defining (within the meta-model) that every Object Type instantiates any number of Object instances. Such a definition is expressed in Fig. 2.4.

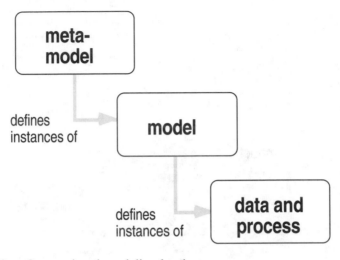

Figure 2.2.   Conventional modeling levels.

The example in Fig. 2.1 would allow Product Type to have instances, such as Sony CD Player and B&O Turntable, at the model level. This would allow object types at the data and process level, for example Sony CD Player, to have instances like "V4572870" and "V4572871." In other words, by defining the instantiates function at the meta-model level, all levels can have types and instances. In fact, the only difference between the model and meta-model levels is that one has instances of the other. Why have these boundaries at all? If one person's object is another person's object type, rigidly maintaining separate levels of abstraction is not always in our best interest.

Modeling in One Framework

As seen above, modeling in rigid, physically separate levels can create problems. These can be remedied by modeling within a single framework instead. In this way:

- Model maintenance is performed on one coherent and integrated model, not fragmented by levels.
- Object types and instances share the same model, so that a two-way knowledge of their association is not lost as they were with segregated levels.
- Any number of instantiates "levels" is possible since a rigid number of levels is not required.

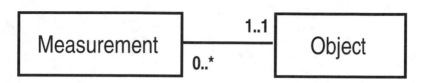

Figure 2.3.   Instances from both model and meta-model levels.

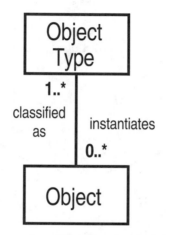

Figure 2.4.   Each instance of an Object Type instantiates any number of Objects; each Object instance is classified as one or more Object Types.

Such an approach has another major advantage. A single framework model can be used to describe itself, as well as, the enterprise. If a model is sufficiently descriptive, it should be able to specify its own object types. A small subset of the model can then describe a much larger subset, which can be propagated to an even larger subset, and so on. Furthermore, any changes to the model can be rigorously specified by and within the model. If a model can be a meta-model to describe itself, it can be a meta-model to describe other models. An approach of this kind can both describe different models and provide a common framework for expressing and comparing models.

Figure 2.5 illustrates this idea. The kernel subset with which the model describes itself would contain such "primitive" object types as Object Type, Object, Relation, and Mapping. In order to support processing requirements, it would also contain object types such as Operation, Trigger Rule, Control Condition, and Event Type. These primitives can be used to form foundational constructs for other structures—which may be used, in turn, as constructs. From here, thinking in terms of meta-models, models, and

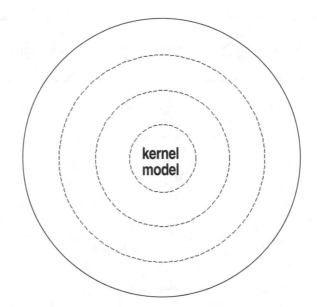

Figure 2.5.   Single framework modeling.

instances is a personal choice. As mentioned earlier, the conceptual and physical boundaries between these are tenuous. In a single framework model, the boundaries are nonexistent. The only reason for inhibiting changes to the hyper-level or meta-level is maintaining standardization.

Meta-Modeling and OOPLs

In short, meta-modeling is an important aspect of modeling objects and their types. Its usefulness is not limited to specifying the enterprise repository and data warehouses. Many application systems will require object types to be objects—and objects to be object types. The OO approach not only supports this, it encourages it. Implementing meta-models in OOPLs, however, is not always straightforward. For example, while ObjVlisp can support it, C++ (for the most part) cannot. Direct meta-modeling support should definitely be an area of future enhancement in both CASE and OOPLs.

CONCLUSION

Meta-models permit us to define a hierarchy of instances. In particular, they permit us to define hierarchies of *types* of objects. For example in Fig. 2.6, Jane is an instance of Human and Property Owner. None of these items is

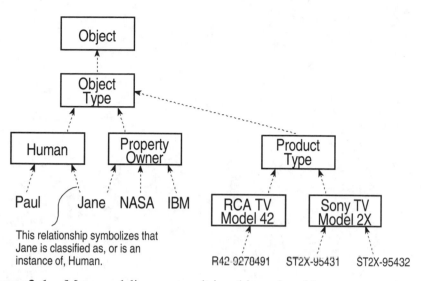

Figure 2.6. Meta-modeling can result in a hierarchy of instances.

a meta-type, because a meta-type has instances that are types. In this way, Object Type, Object, and Product Type are meta-types. For most programmers this is foreign thinking. However, for builders of CASE tools, repositories, and data warehouses, this a common and necessary way of thinking.

Power Types

May 1994

G rouping the various objects in our world by categories, or types, is
an important technique we employ to organize and understand our
world. In several approaches to object-oriented analysis, the term *object
type* refers to categories of objects. For instance, the object type Employee
refers to a category of people who have an employment relationship with
one or more organizations. Typically, we use object diagrams to represent
the various types of objects and their relationships in our systems. However,
a particularly complex expression of categorization called *power types* is
not addressed by traditional object-structure approaches. Most systems
have numerous *power types,* which are either unnoticed or misunderstood.
This chapter addresses the following questions:

- What are power types?
- Why are power types so important?
- What are some common examples of power types?
- How can power types be represented?

INTRODUCTION TO THE NEED FOR POWER TYPES

As mentioned above, grouping the objects in our world by categories, or
types, is an important technique for us. For instance, one of the ways
botanists organize trees is by species. In this way, each tree we see can be
classified as an American elm, sugar maple, apricot, saguaro—or some
other species of tree. Figure 3.1 illustrates this idea. The circle on the left
depicts various instances of the object type Tree. For example, one of these
instances could be the tree in your front yard, the tree in your neighbor's

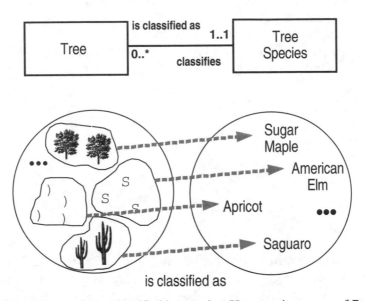

Figure 3.1.   Trees can be classified by species. Here are instances of Trees classified as particular Tree Species.

backyard, or trees at your local nursery. The circle on the right contains instances of Tree Species, such as sugar maple and apricot. Furthermore, this figure indicates the relationships that exist between these two sets of objects. For example, the tree in your front yard might be classified as a sugar maple, your neighbor's tree as an apricot, and so on.

The object diagram at the top of Fig. 3.1 expresses that each Tree Species classifies zero or more Trees, and each Tree is classified as exactly one Tree Species. Figure 3.2 supplements this by including additional relationships with Tree and Tree Species. Here, each Tree Species is identified using a Leaf Pattern and is generally found in any number of Geographic Locations. For example, the saguaro cactus has leaves reduced to large spines and is generally found in southern Arizona and northern Sonora. Additionally, this figure indicates each Tree is found in a particular Geographic Location. In this way, a particular tree could be classified as a saguaro and be located in Phoenix, Arizona.

Figure 3.3 depicts another object diagram involving trees. Here, Tree is subtyped as being a American Elm, Sugar Maple, Apricot, or Saguaro—or something else. Furthermore, each subtype has its own specialized properties. For instance, each Sugar Maple has yearly maple sugar yield of some given Quantity Measure, each Saguaro is inhabited by zero or more instances of a Gila Woodpecker, and so on.

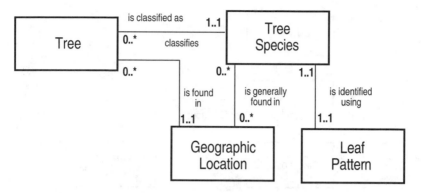

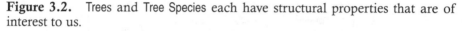

Figure 3.2. Trees and Tree Species each have structural properties that are of interest to us.

Which Diagram is Correct?

Figure 3.2 models a relationship type between Trees and Tree Species. Figure 3.3, on the other hand, expresses species of trees as subtypes of Tree. In other words, both model the fact that trees have species in different ways. The common question asked by many analysts is which diagram should be used to model trees and their species.

The diagram in Fig. 3.2 is useful for several reasons. First, it indicates that each Tree Species possesses unique properties, such as its indicative leaf pattern and general habitat. Since every instance of Tree Species possesses these properties, a Tree Species object type is useful to express such relationships with Leaf Pattern and Geographic Location. Secondly, the Tree Species object type provides a mechanism for maintaining an organized collection of tree species. For instance, if a new tree species is identified, it becomes a member of the Tree Species object type. If a tree species is removed, it is deleted as a member. The Tree Species object type, therefore, contains our list of valid tree species. Furthermore, changing that list does not require us to change the object diagram. Lastly, indicating that individual trees are classified by species, without listing every possible species, is graphically economical. North America alone has nearly 850 species of trees. Depicting all of these species as subtypes of Tree would be overwhelming. The classification relationship between Tree and Tree Species means that somebody will populate the collections of Tree and Tree Species (and the associations between the two) without representing the instances on an object diagram.

Figure 3.3, on the other hand, is also useful. It permits us to express properties that are appropriate for only specialized kinds of trees. For

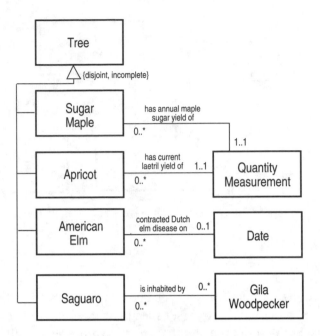

Figure 3.3.   Trees can be subtyped into species. Such subtypes are useful when they exhibit different kinds of properties from Trees in general.

example, maintaining the date that a particular American elm contracted Dutch elm disease is not appropriate for any other species of tree in North America. Therefore, placing a contracted Dutch Elm disease on Date association on the Tree object type would be imprecise. Placing such an association on the American Elm subtype of Tree would be more logical. In this way, *only* instances of American Elm may have a contracted Dutch elm disease on Date association.

Since the diagrams in Figs. 3.2 and 3.3 are both useful, choosing to use only one presents a problem. By choosing only one diagram, the properties of the other are lost. If the approach depicted in Fig. 3.2 is chosen, the benefits of Tree subtypes and their specialized properties expressed in Fig. 3.3 are lost. If the opposite approach is chosen, the ability to express properties of species is lost. A logical conclusion is to use *both* forms—either as separate diagrams or as one diagram illustrated in Fig. 3.4.

What if Both Diagrams are Used?

If both forms are used, the issue of maintaining integrity must be addressed. For instance, if botanists got together and decided that the American elm should no longer be a species of tree, the American elm object would then

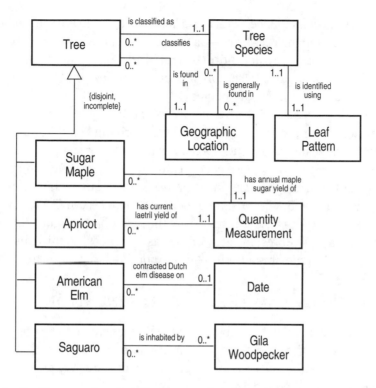

Figure 3.4. Trees can be classified by species. Here are instances of Trees classified as particular Tree Species.

be removed as an instance of Tree Species. To maintain the integrity of our model in such a situation, the American Elm subtype of Tree must also be removed. Additionally, if a new species were added as a subtype of Tree, that new species would have to be added as an instance of Tree Species. The same kind of situation exists if the name of a tree species were changed—both the subtype of Tree and the instance of Tree Species would have to be modified accordingly.

Species are Species

As it turns out, the different modeling approaches depicted above are not really all that different. In reality, the subtypes of Tree and the instances of Tree Species are the same objects. In other words, the subtypes of Tree in Fig. 3.2 *are* instances of Tree Species. Furthermore, the instances of Tree Species in Fig. 3.1 *are* the subtypes of Tree in Fig. 3.2. The fact that there is an instance of Tree Species called Sugar Maple and a subtype of Tree called

Sugar Maple is no coincidence. Sugar Maple and Sugar Maple are the *same* object. The instances of Tree Species are—as the name implies—*types* of trees. The subtypes of Tree are—by definition—*types* of trees. While Tree may be partitioned in various ways (based on size or age, for example), in Fig. 3.2 it is partitioned on the basis of species.

In short, Figs. 3.2 and 3.3 are two ways of *modeling* trees and their species. Furthermore, the models are based on the underlying fact that the subtypes of Tree and the instances of Tree Species are the same objects. Therefore, the integrity issue mentioned above is not really an issue here. Deleting the American Elm subtype from the Tree partition does not require also deleting the corresponding Tree Species instance, because the American Elm subtype and the corresponding Tree Species instance are the *same* object. Figure 3.5 expresses another way of representing subtypes as instances. While this is not a "standard" technique, it is a useful—if temporary—communication device.

POWER TYPES AND THEIR REPRESENTATION

As established above, the instances of object types can also be object types. (This is the stuff that meta-models are made of.) These same instances, however, can also be *subtypes* of another object type. When this occurs, we have what is called a *power type*.

> A *power type* is an object type whose instances are subtypes of another object type.

In the examples above, Tree Species is a power type for the Tree object type. Therefore, the instances of Tree Species are subtypes of Tree. This concept applies to many situations within many lines of business. Figure 3.6 depicts examples of other power types. The double-arrow symbol in the middle of the line points *to* the power type and *away* from the object type being subtyped. In this way, the diagram in Fig. 3.6(a) can be interpreted as "each instance of Account is classified with exactly one instance of Account Type." It can also be interpreted as "the instances of Account Type are subtypes of Account."

Associating Power Types and Subtype Partitions

Figure 3.6(a) represents the set of subtypes for Account. Instead of thinking of this as just a set of subtypes, think of this as a collection of objects. The

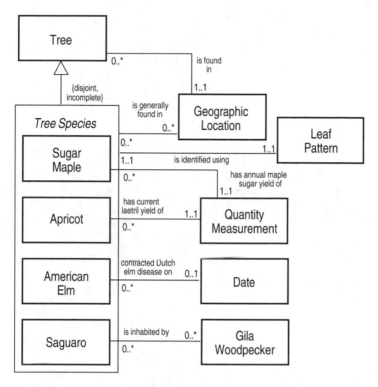

Figure 3.5. Treating the powertype as the partition is not standard. In reality, the Tree Species box can be thought of as a symbol for the Tree Species object type.

underlying theme of this collection is that it contains *types* of Accounts. In other words, it contains Account Types. Here, it is reasonably obvious that the subtypes in the partition are instances of Account Type.

In Fig. 3.7, each subtype partitioning is labeled with the name of the power type to which it relates. For example, the partition on the right is labeled Insurance Line. This means that the object types in this partition are instances of Insurance Line. This approach is beneficial because it reduces the number of lines on a diagram.

Labeling partitions becomes increasing important when a power type is expressed with multiple partitions. For instance, in Fig. 3.7 a Policy can be subtyped as either a Life, Health, Property/Casualty, or some other Insurance Line. Furthermore, a Property/Casualty policy can be further subtyped as Automobile, Equipment, Inland Marine, or some other Property/Casualty line of insurance. In other words, the subtypes in the partitions labeled Insurance Line are all instances of the Insurance Line power type.

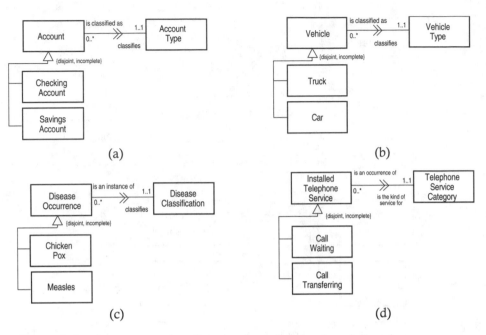

(a)   (b)

(c)   (d)

Figure 3.6.   Some examples of power types from various industries.

Power Types versus Subtype Partitions

Does this mean that every time a subtype partition is defined, a power type should also exist—or vice versa? For example in Fig. 3.8, Employee is partitioned in being a Female Employee and a Male Employee. Insisting that every subtype partition have a power type would mean that Employee should have a power type of Employee Gender Type. By the same reasoning, the presence of a Job Classification power type would also require a subtype partition containing all of the various job classes, such as Junior Programmer, Intermediate Clerk Typist, Senior Machinist, and Principal Guru. Yet, the Employee Gender Type and the subtypes of Job Classification are not represented in Fig. 3.8. (Since no subtypes for Job Classification are represented on this diagram, some analysts would not consider indicating it as a power type of Employee at all. However, expressing the power type here suggests the potential for representing subtypes on other diagrams—or on this diagram in the future.)

Such omissions are not *necessarily* flaws in analysis. If such object types have no structural or behavioral features that specialize them in any way, they are—by definition—not useful. In other words, this diagram implies that Employee Gender Type and Senior Machinist have no features other than those that apply because of some supertype. If the analyst constructing this

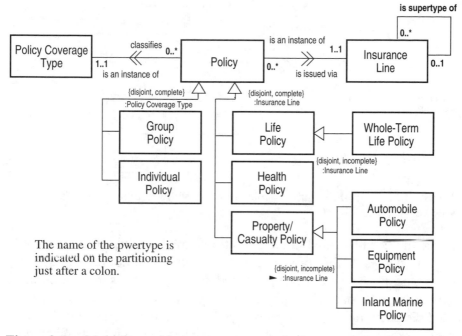

Figure 3.7.   Multiple partitions may represent the instances of a single power type. Here, multiple subtyping levels are expressed.

diagram decides that Intermediate Clerk Typists have one or more properties *in addition* to those that already apply to every Employee, Intermediate Clerk Typist would appear on this diagram. If the analyst constructing this diagram decides that the instances of Employee Gender Type have one or more properties *in addition* to those that apply to every Object Type, Employee Gender Type would be represented. In short, power types imply the existence of subtype partitions and subtype partitions imply the existence of power types. However, subtype and power types should only be represented when they are useful for modeling the problem at hand. If they have structural or behavioral features that specialize them in some way, they are useful. Depicting unuseful concepts just adds noise. The good analyst will express just what is needed—and not one more thing.

Implementing Power Types

Implementing power types can present challenges for the average environment. To implement power types with a relational database would mean that the instances of a relation could also be relations in their own

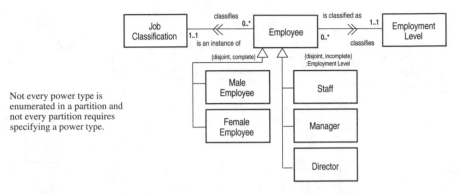

Not every power type is enumerated in a partition and not every partition requires specifying a power type.

Figure 3.8. Partitions may or may not have power types represented—and vice versa.

right. In object-oriented implementations, the instances of a class could also be classes. If the software implementation can not directly support classes being objects and vice versa, redundant structures must be defined. For each new instance of a power type class, a new class must also be created. For each instance of a power type class that is deleted, the appropriate class must also be deleted. Maintaining integrity in this kind of situation, then, is vital—but feasible nonetheless. Power types are a conceptual, or analysis, notion. They express a real world situation. If the power type is to be implemented in a system, the task may not be easy and efficient. However, the software designer must be aware of power types, because they are a common phenomenon.

SUMMARY

Grouping the various objects in our world by categories, or types, is an important technique we employ to organize and understand our world. In several approaches to object-oriented analysis, the term *object type* refers to categories of objects. Typically, we use object diagrams to represent the various types of objects and their relationships in our systems. However, a particularly complex expression of categorization called *power types* is not addressed by traditional object structure approaches. A power type is an object type whose instances are subtypes of another object type. Most systems have many power types, but they are either unnoticed or misunderstood.

Specifying Structural Constraints

October 1993

W e know that objects exist in our world, that objects relate to one another, and that these objects and their associations can be changed. However, certain restrictions can also exist that limit the way objects relate and the way changes can occur. Such restrictions are called *constraints.* A constraint is a property that is either true or false. Constraints are always expected to be true [Gray, 1992] and are usually categorized as being *structural* or *behavioral* in nature.

- *Structural constraints* limit the way objects associate with each other, that is, they restrict object state.
- *Behavioral constraints* limit the way object state changes may occur.

This column explores structural constraints and, in particular, focuses on answering the following questions:

- How can cardinality constraints be extended to go beyond the traditional zero, one, or many?
- What are the implications of constraining an association that maps to *bags, sets,* and *ordering?*
- How can the order of objects of the same type be restricted?
- Can an association have more than one constraint?
- What about uniqueness and invariant constraints?
- While there are many common constraints, can constraints also be customized?

ZERO, ONE, AND MANY CARDINALITIES

The objects of one type can be assigned, or *mapped,* to objects of another type. Furthermore, the number of objects mapped can be restricted. With this in mind, Fig. 4.1 can be read: via the employs mapping, every Employer object maps to one or more Person objects. For instance, Employer 1 employs Bob and Carol, Employer 2 employs Ted, and so on. Inversely, each Person optionally maps to an Employer, and if it does, it maps to one Employer at most. For instance, Ted is employed by Employer 2, Alice is not employed, and so on.

The restriction of how many objects must map from one type to another is called a *cardinality constraint.* (In UML, this is known as *multiplicity.*) The maximum, or upper bound, cardinality constraint is most often expressed in terms of mapping an object to one or to some undefined "many" objects. In addition, the minimum, or lower bound, cardinality constraint is most often expressed as zero or one. The zero indicates that each object *may* not map to any object at all. The one indicates that each object *must* map to least one object.

BEYOND ZERO, ONE, AND MANY CARDINALITIES

In addition to zero, one, and many, other cardinality constraints are possible. For example in Fig. 4.2(a), the upper bound on the has biological parents cardinality is not zero, one, or many. Instead, the mapping is constrained to map to no more than two biological parents. Here, the lower bound is set to zero, because this diagram models the reality of most businesses. In other words, while nature may require a 2..2 cardinality constraint, businesses should not. For a business to require the knowledge of a person's parents—who in turn have two parents, each with two more parents, and so on—would be an exponential activity. In this example, a lower bound of zero could be specified simply because the knowledge is not required, the information may not always be known, it avoids Genesis-level conflicts, or a combination of other reasons.*

Figure 4.2(b) depicts another example of a cardinality constraint that is not zero, one, or many. In this figure, a particular organization has determined

---

* As characterized by Tom Cairns, a physician for the National Health Service in London, the analyst must choose to model from one of three perspectives: how it is, how the analyst would like it to be, or on the basis of what can be recorded.

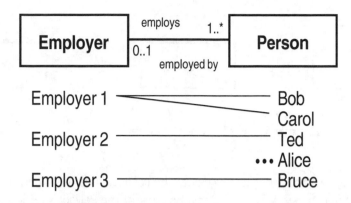

Figure 4.1. Examples of zero, one, and many cardinality constraints.

that each Meeting must have at least 2 Persons but cannot exceed 20 Persons. (Mappings beyond 20 persons might be considered an Assembly instead.) This technique applies to many modeling situations, such as the number of players on a cricket team must be 11.

Until now, cardinality constraints have been specified solely in terms of a minimum and maximum value. However, other ways of specifying cardinality constraints exist. In Fig. 4.3(a) for instance, a particular tennis tournament may require each tennis game be played with either 2 or 4 persons (that is, a singles or a doubles game). Mappings can also be restricted to an odd or even number of objects. For example, any number of people can participate in a 2-legged race, but in Fig. 4.3(b) a 3-legged race must have an even number of participants. Another constraint might specify that only a prime number of relatable objects are allowed or that the number of permitted objects can even be derived as necessary. Such precise information needs to be formally documented, because it defines and determines the organization.

CONSTRAINTS TO ORDER MAPPING

Mappings can be constrained in ways other than by cardinality. For example, Fig. 4.4 depicts three ways in which the association between an object and *collections* of objects can be constrained. Figure 4.4(a) specifies that a Polygon is connected via 3 or more points. Within the curly brackets that indicate mapping constraints is an additional constraint—ordered. The ordered constraint means that the mapping to this collection of objects occurs in a

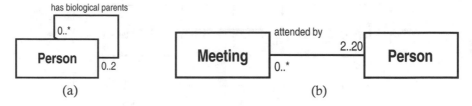

Figure 4.2.   Enumerated cardinality constraints.

fixed order. In this way, a Polygon can be connected via a collection of Points in a specified order. Without such a constraint the Polygon's perimeter could not be known. It would be like the children's game of connect-the-dots. Without a defined sequence for connecting the dots, the intended image might never emerge.

CONSTRAINTS ON MAPPING TO DUPLICATE OBJECTS (BAGS)

Sometimes an object can map to the same object more than once. For example, Fig. 4.4(b) specifies that a Patient complains of one or more Problems. The bag constraint indicates that the mapping results in a collection that may contain *duplicate* objects. In this example, a Patient can complain about the same problem more than once. Chances are, the OO programmer may wish to timestamp these associations to record the basis for the apparent duplication. In any case, the bag constraint just ensures that the knowledge of duplication is not lost. The bag constraint is not generally used by analysts, because duplication is not usually allowed. The set constraint, on the other hand, is so common that it is the accepted default.

CONSTRAINTS ON MAPPINGS WHERE DUPLICATES ARE NOT ALLOWED (SETS)

In a bag, the same object may appear any number of times. In a set, an object may appear only once. For example, Fig. 4.4(c) specifies that an Organization employs any number of Persons. The set constraint indicates the mapping results in a collection that contains no duplicate objects. A particular Person, then, may appear only once for any given Organization. In other words, while each Person may be employed by *multiple* Organizations, that same Person cannot be an employee of a given Organization more than once.

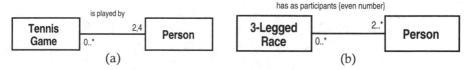

Figure 4.3.   Constraint with enumerated cardinalities.

Again, the set constraint is such a common mapping constraint that it need not be explicitly stated—but treated as a default.

CONSTRAINING THE ORDER OF OBJECTS (TREE, LATTICE, AND SO ON)

As discussed above, the ordered constraint restricts the way a mapping is sequenced from one object type to another. However, a single object type can *appear* to have a certain *internal* order among its instances. Here, objects of the same type relate to one another in a particular way. For example, Fig. 4.5(a) expresses that sub/supertype hierarchies are subject to the lattice constraint (sometimes called the directed acyclic graph, or DAG, constraint instead). Here, the cardinality constraint permits an object type to have any number of subtypes and supertypes. The lattice constraint, however, restricts the association even further. It ensures that the same object type cannot be *both* the subtype and supertype of another object type.

If used in Fig. 4.5(b), the lattice constraint would ensure that an employee's boss cannot also report to that employee. Furthermore, to ensure that an employee cannot have more than one boss, the cardinality constraint specifies that each Employee may be managed by 0 or 1 other Employees. However, this also means that Employees are not required to have a boss at all. If permitted, such a situation could quickly render an organization ineffective. Yet, to enforce *every* Employee to have a boss would create a different problem. Even the top boss would require a boss—resulting in an infinite chain of bosses. In short, such structures require more than just cardinality and lattice constraints. Figure 4.5(b), therefore, specifies that this hierarchy be a tree structure. Tree constraints ensure that, while a tree may have many branches, it may only have *one* root. In this way, every Employee has a boss *except one.**

---

* Specifying a lattice instead of a tree constraint in Fig. 4.5(b) would permit *multiple* roots—being, in effect, a multiple tree constraint. This is why tree structures are also known as a rooted lattice or rooted DAG.

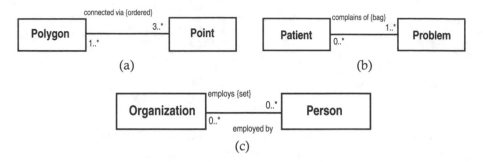

Figure 4.4.   Constraints on mapping to collections.

Figure 4.5 illustrates two kinds of ordering constraints. Ordering can also be restricted in other ways, such as chain and cyclic constraints. Furthermore, since the effect of every ordering is bidirectional, it constrains both the mapping *and* its inverse. In Fig. 4.5(a), the manages and the managed by mappings are both subject to the tree constraint, that is, the relationship itself is constrained. Therefore, declaring an ordering constraint anywhere on the relationship line indicates that the ordering constrains both the mapping and its inverse. Such relationships are also referred to as *ordering relationships* [Langer, 1967]. Ordering relationships constrain the way in which objects of a particular type relate to each other.

COMMON RELATIONSHIP CONSTRAINTS

Relationships have some of the same relational constraints that are common in mathematics. For example, they can be reflexive, irreflexive, symmetric, asymmetric, antisymmetric, transitive, and nontransitive. With a reflexive constraint, objects are free to relate to other objects—as long the object relates to itself as well. For instance, the is as old as mapping in Fig. 4.6(a) is reflexive. Here, Persons can be as old as any number of other people, but are always as old as themselves. The irreflexive constraint does not permit reflexive associations. For instance, the is mother of mapping is irreflexive because no Person can be their own mother.

Symmetric relationships are those where the meaning of a mapping is the same as its inverse. For example, the is spouse of mapping has the same meaning in reverse. Whereas, the asymmetric constraint does not permit symmetry. The is wife of mapping is one example, because the is husband of would be the correct inverse. Antisymmetric is a constraint that permits a

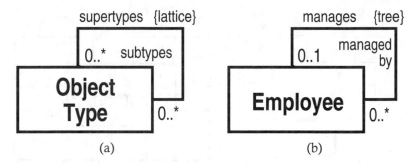

Figure 4.5. A lattice constraint on the Object Type sub/supertype hierarchy and a tree constraint on an Employee management hierarchy.

symmetric relationship only if the two objects being related are the *same* object. For instance, the is present at the birth of is antisymmetric because only you can be present at your own birth (as long as we don't allow twins).

Transitive relationships ensure, for example, that if Bob is an ancestor of Bart and Bart is an ancestor of Bubba, then Bob must also be an ancestor of Bubba. The absence of this constraint means that transitivity cannot be assumed. For example, if Betty is a client of Beth and Beth is a client of Beatrice, then Betty is *not necessarily* a client of Bubba.

For the constraints mentioned so far, the relationships have indicated only single constraints. Nevertheless, multiple constraints can be represented. For instance, the is a client of association in Fig. 4.6(a) is specified as being both asymmetric and irreflexive. Representing every constraint on every relationship, however, will prove cumbersome. To reduce this burden, certain default constraints can be assumed. For instance, in the absence of a common relationship constraint, an irreflexive and asymmetric association can be assumed. Just remember, by formally specifying those constraints required by the business, you communicate clearly to the system implementors. With code generators, their implementation can be automated *from the diagram*.

OTHER STRUCTURAL CONSTRAINTS

The mapping constraints presented in this column are by no means *all* of the forms that can be employed in OO analysis. There are many constraints that are commonly used. For instance, mappings are considered to be invariant if their instances cannot be changed once they are created. Uniqueness constraints ensure that a mapping, or a combination of mappings, provide unique identification for a given type of object.

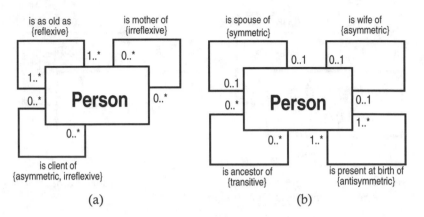

(a)   (b)

Figure 4.6. Examples of common relationship constraints on relationships between people.

Additionally, the analyst and user can specify their own mapping constraints. For instance, Fig. 4.7 illustrates two such rules. The curly bracketed text at the top of the diagram constrains the insures mapping (with ramifications for constraints on the benefits mapping). Instead of writing out the whole rule, the is effective for mapping is constrained by some predefined Rule 22.

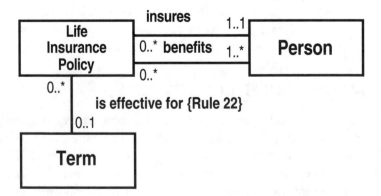

Figure 4.7. The analyst and user can specify their own mapping constraints.

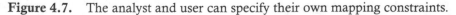

REFERENCES

Gray, Peter M. D., Krishnarao G. Kulkarni, and Norman W. Paton, *Object-Oriented Databases: A Semantic Data Model Approach,* Prentice-Hall, New York, 1992.

Langer, Susanne K., *An Introduction to Symbolic Logic,* (3rd edition), Dover Publications, New York, 1967.

Toward a Formalization of OO Analysis

James J. Odell and Guus Ramackers

July 1997

INTRODUCTION

While there are many books on OO analysis, few formalize their underlying notions. For most practitioners, this is not a problem. However, building meta-CASE tools, defining repository structures, and comparing OO notations requires an exacting approach. Everything must be clear and unambiguous. One way to ensure a clarity of ideas is through mathematical formalism. This paper is an initial attempt to produce such a formalism for those notions used to represent the results of OO analysis.

To begin with, analysis and design are defined as follows:

> *Analysis* is a process that maps from a perception of the real world to a representation.
>
> *Design* is a process that maps from an analysis representation to an expression of implementation, that is, from a problem to a solution.

The two are different, because perception and its eventual implementation may—and usually do—differ. For instance, during a business process reengineering (BPR) activity, a domain expert may have her own notion of how order processing can or should be performed without prejudice for implementation. It is the designer's task to determine the most appropriate implementation using the currently available technology—including restriction, changes, and additions required to support the selected implementation. Again, this paper addresses the formalization of OO within analysis. Furthermore, it deals with the structural rather than the behavioral notions of objects. (It discusses the "universe of objects" rather than the character of objects as they may change over time.)

CONCEPTS

Due to its conceptual nature, a fundamental notion in analysis is the term concept.

> A *concept* is an idea or notion that we apply to classify those things around us.

As Susan Langer puts it, "we are consciously, deliberately abstracting the form from all the things which have it. Such an abstracted form is called a concept." [Langer, 1967] For instance, if we list all those things to which the concept "being a mortal" applies, we would form the set of all mortals. Concepts, then, have two important aspects—*intension* and *extension* [Whitehead, 1910; Russell, 1938].

> The *intension* of a concept is its meaning, or its complete definition.
>
> The *extension* of a concept is the collection, or *set,* of things to which the concept applies.

For example, the intension of the concept Mortal could be stated as "anything that dies." The extension of the concept Mortal, then, would be the collection, or *set**, of things to which the definition applies. This example could also be expressed in the following manner:

$\forall x : (x \text{ must die}) \Rightarrow (x \in \text{Mortal})$.

---

* Some authors prefer the word *class* instead of *set*. Due to the overloaded usage of the word *class,* this paper will use *set,* instead.

This expression says that for any x, if x must die, then x is a member of the set of Mortal objects. For example, if "Socrates must die" is true, then Socrates belongs to the set of Mortal objects. The set of Mortal objects, therefore, is not a fixed collection. It is defined by a propositional form, not by its specific members. In short, if we understand the intension, we are acquainted with the extension—even if we have never seen an individual that belongs to it. (For example, we may possess the concept of Unicorn without ever seeing an instance of one.) However, the converse is not necessarily true. If we understand the extension, we do not necessarily know the intension. For example, a set D might contain my pencil, an eraser, and a pad of paper. Here, the intension of D is not clear. Yet, if I define the concept D as all those things currently placed on my office desk, we understand the extension.

As demonstrated above, intensions determine whether or not a given object is a member of an extension. As such, they can be readily expressed as elementary propositions. Every elementary proposition has a truth-value, which is either true or false. In real life, we are not always able to fully formalize our intensions in predicate logic. In these kinds of situations, automated systems would require human intervention to assert whether or not a given object is a Person. For those kinds of situations where the intension can be formalized, automating a concept's definition in program code is possible. In contrast, formalizing a concept's extension is much easier. Here, a set-theoretic approach can be used.

In this paper, concept(C) will refer to the concept of C. The intension of C will be expressed as int(C), and the extension as ext(C). For example, the intension of the concept of Mortal could be represented as

int(Mortal) = $\forall x : (x$ must die$)$.

The extension of the concept of Mortal could be represented as

ext(Mortal) = {Socrates, Plato}.

CLASSIFICATION RELATIONS

To say that an object o is *classified* as a concept C, then, means that both

- the intension of C is "true" for the object o, and
- the object o is a *member* of the extension of C.

This paper will represent the *classification* relation with the symbol "$\in$".*
So that $o \in C$ means that the concept C applies to the thing o. Inversely,
the thing o is an *instance* of the concept C.

As discussed above, each concept has two aspects. When considering a
concept "in extension," the relation $\in$ can also be used to indicate membership when the concept is qualified as such. For example, to express that
Socrates is a member of the Mortal set could be represented as

> Socrates $\in$ ext(Mortal).

Expressing a classification relation from an intensional perspective, a similar technique can be used. Since this paper will deal primarily with the
extensional nature of concepts, the "ext" qualifier will be removed for ease
of readability from this point on. Therefore, an alternate way to represent
Socrates $\in$ ext(Mortal) is

> Socrates $\in$ Mortal.

Finally, to bring the terminology of this paper in line with accepted
usage by the OMG, ANSI, and ISO, a few words must be changed. The
term *concept* must be changed to *type,* and the word *thing* to *object.* These
terms are expressed formally:

Object is defined as the first element (or left side) of the
classification relation.

Type is defined as the last element (or right side) of the
classification relation.

In other words, an object is defined as an instance of a type. A type is
defined as a concept—where the membership of the type is a set based on
the intension of the type. The terms *instance* and *object,* then, can be used
synonymously.

---

* In this paragraph, $\in$ implies both intension and extension. Since $\in$ is often thought of solely in terms of set membership, some use the ! symbol as a more general representation. In
this situation, $o ! C$ would mean that the concept C applies to the value o—implying both
intension and extension.

Design Considerations

As defined above, types are free from implementation considerations. Implementing a type could require multiple OO *classes*—or non-OO constructions such as relational tables or business rules. Furthermore, a class may implement more than one type. Since implementations of types are not one for one with classes, types and classes are not the same. *Classes,* then, are defined as OO implementations of concepts, or types.

While OMG, ANSI, and ISO differentiate between type and class as defined above, the term object is used for both conceptual and implementation instances. In analysis, the term object is defined as an instance of a type. In design, object is defined as an instance of a class.

However, the properties of an object will differ between analysis and design usages. For example in OODB design, every object must have a permanent, unique object identifier, or *OID*. Analysis, however, requires no such property. In analysis, permanent unique identity is required only when our perception of the real world requires it. For example, car manufacturers require every vehicle to have a permanent unique vehicle identifier. However, these same manufacturers will *not* require permanent unique identity for each of its nuts and bolts. In other words, while each nut and bolt is unique, identifiers are not required. In contrast, OO programmers always require permanent unique identity because OO languages require it.

Similarly, the classification relation requires no specific implementation. It only asserts that a given object is an instance of a given type. To support the classification relation in an OO programming language, every object usually contains a pointer or reference to the class that constructed it.

GENERALIZATION/SPECIALIZATION RELATIONS

> Any type *A,* each of whose objects is also an instance of a given type *S,* is called a specialization (or *subtype*) of *S* and is written as $A \subset S$. *S* is also called the generalization (or *supertype*) of *A*.

As with the classification relation the specialization relation can also be qualified in extensional and intensional terms. For example,

ext(Human) $\subset$ ext(Mortal), or simply, Human $\subset$ Mortal means that every member of the Human set is also a member of the Mortal set. In contrast,

int(Human) ⊂ int(Mortal)

means the definition of Human must contain the definition of Mortal. When viewed in extension, the left side of the ⊂ involves fewer than the right, because the left side (by definition) is a subset. When viewed in intension, the left side of the ⊂ involves more than the right, because the definition of the left must also include the definition of the right. In short, when going down a generalization hierarchy, the extension gets smaller while the intension gets bigger. For example, the intension of being Human must involve being Mortal, whereas the intension of being Mortal does *not* involve being Human. In this way, ⊂ really means *inclusion,* that is, the concept of Human is *included in* the concept of Mortal.* Inclusion, therefore, refers to both extension and intension. As with the classification relation, extension and intension can be addressed separately by qualification (as indicated in the examples above).

Design Considerations

With generalization/specialization, the OO analyst would tend to read the expression, Employee ⊂ Human, as "every Employee is also a Human" or that "Employee is a subtype of Human." In other words, being in the Employee set implies being in the Human set, or being an Employee also involves what it takes to be a Human. In contrast, an OO programmer would instead say something like "Employees *inherit* the structure and behavior of Humans." Inheritance, however, is one—of several—*implementations* of generalization. (For other implementations of generalization, see Chapter 12 in [Martin/Odell, 1996].) The analyst, who is supposed to think implementation-free, only knows that whatever *applies* to Humans also *applies* to Employees. *How* the properties of a type get applied to its subtypes is an implementation problem, not a conceptual one. In short, generalization expresses *what* and inheritance expresses *how.*

RELATIONS IN GENERAL

The Cartesian product $S \times T$ of two sets S and T is the set of all ordered pairs

---

* Since ⊂ is often thought of solely in terms of set membership, some use the < symbol as a more general representation. So that $B < C$ means that the concept B is *included* is the concept C—implying both intension and extension.

(a,b) with a ∈ S and b ∈ T. The instances of a Cartesian product are called *tuples*.*

> A relation $\mathfrak{R}$ on sets S and T is a subset of the Cartesian product $S \times T$. $\mathfrak{R}$ is said to hold for the ordered pair (a,b) and can be written in the form $\mathfrak{R}\,(a,b)$.[†]

For example, an employment relation on sets Person and Company can be written Employment Contract(Person, Company) and have the following tuples:

Person	Company
Bob	NASA
Bob	IBM
Betty	IBM
Bernard	NEC
...	...

By definition, each tuple in a relation is an object, because it is an instance of the ordered pair for which the relation holds. In the above example, the tuple (Bob, NASA) is an object because it is an instance of the Employment Contract relation. In other words, it can be written, (Bob, NASA) ∈ Employment Contract, where Employment Contract holds for the ordered pair (Person, Company). Furthermore, since the Employment relation has instances (albeit tuples), Employment Contract is a type—by definition.

Since each relation is also a type, its extension may be a set that participates in another Cartesian product—and, therefore, another relation. For example, every instance of an Employment Contract could be assigned to one or more offices for that person's employment (where each office may in turn have one or more employees). Here, such an office-assignment can be defined as a relation on the set of tuples defined by Employment Contract(Person, Company) and a set of Office objects. This can be written

Office Assignment((Employment Contract(Person, Company)), Office)

or abbreviated

Office Assignment(Employment Contract, Office)

---

* The instances of a Cartesian product of n sets is called an *n-tuple*.
[†] A relation on multiple sets can be written $\mathfrak{R}\,(a,b,...)$.

and have the following tuples:

Person	Company	Office
(Bob	NASA)	#099
(Bob	IBM)	#123
(Betty	IBM)	#123
(Betty	IBM)	#224
(Bernard	NEC)	#345
...	...	...

The instances of Office Assignment, too, may have relationships with other sets. For example, each Office Assignment could have an effective date for the office assignment and be expressed as

Assignment Effectivity(Office Assignment((Employment Contract(
   Person, Company)), Office), Date).

Any relation, then, can in turn define a set for other relations. In other words, for any relation $\mathfrak{R}$ on sets S and $T,$ S and T can define collections of "simple" objects or "complex" (tuple) objects. Both are instances of sets—and therefore may paired using the Cartesian product. A common term used by the OO community for relations is relationship types.

The term *relationship type* is synonymous with *relation*.

Design Considerations

Implementing relations, or relationship types, requires more thought. For example, if you are designing for a relational database, relations like Employment Contract would be implemented as a table with its own set of records. If you are designing an OO database, Employment Contract might not necessarily be implemented as a class. For instance, if the Employment Contract relation was *not* part of any order pair, most OO programmers would not implement the relation as a class. The main reason given for this is that such a class would "break" encapsulation. However, when a relation is part of an ordered pair, the relation would be implemented as a class. For example, if Employment Contract became a component of the Office Assignment relation, Employment Contract would become a class, because the Office Assignment relation requires instances to pair. In this case, the instances are a Cartesian product of the Employment Contract and Office classes. However, Office Assignment itself would not become a class unless it, too, furnished objects for another relation, such as Assignment Effectivity.

FUNCTIONS

So far we have employed sets and relations as ways of expressing how we think about objects and their associations. In other words, we can formalize—as well as formally manipulate—objects and associations. Therefore, any mathematical function that can be defined on sets and objects may be used, such as union, intersect, difference, compare, and arithmetic operations. To introduce the notion of function, we can start where we left off—with relations.

With mathematics, we can use certain properties of relations to play particular roles (such as reflexive, symmetric, and transitive). In particular, one relational role is quite useful: the *right unique* relation.

> A relation $\Re$ is right unique when for all $x, y, z \in S$:
> if $\Re(x, y)$ and $\Re(x, z)$, then $y = z$.

This right unique relation provides us with a formal way of expressing the mappings of one set of objects to another. Another name for this mechanism is called the *function*.

> A *function* on a set X with values in Y is a *right unique relation* with support (or domain) in X and range in Y.

A function, then, is the set of all ordered pairs (x,y) of a relation $\Re$, with $x \in X$ and $y \in Y$, where there is a many-to-one correspondence between the members of X and the members of Y. In summary, functions are a special case of relation. Relations are useful when we wish to express associations as instances of pairings, or *tuples*. In contrast, when we are given an object of one set and wish to return, or "navigate" to, an associated object in another set, functions are useful.

Functions in Practice

Figure 5.1 depicts an association between two types: Person and Company. The line associating these two concepts represents the relation Employment Contract, which holds for the ordered pair (Person, Company). As discussed

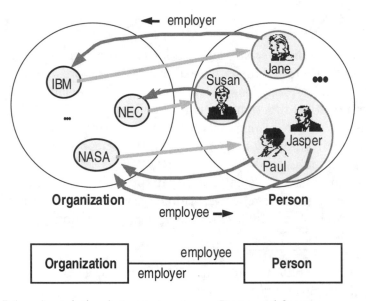

Figure 5.1.   Association between two types: Person and Company.

earlier, the instances of relationship types are called tuples. Therefore, any time a user wishes to create an employment relationship between a person and a company, an Employment Contract tuple may be created.

However, tuples are not sufficient for every application. Often, a user only knows of objects in one set and wishes to obtain objects in a related set. For example, relationally it could be true that Bob and NASA are related as a tuple of Employment Contract; and so is Bob and IBM. In other words, (Bob, NASA) ∈ Employment Contract, and (Bob, IBM) ∈ Employment Contract. However, what if your application wanted to find out who employed Bob? In other words, you possessed an instance in the Person set and wish to determine which object it was related to in the Company set. A function (or right-unique relation) is used to traverse the Cartesian product Person × Company, where the domain is Person and the range is Company. This function is called *employer.* This can be restated in functional terms as, employer(Person) = Company, yielding employer(Betty) = IBM.

This basic approach works fine with Betty but breaks down for Bob who is employed by two companies: NASA and IBM. If the function were evaluated for Bob, two instances would be returned. Since a function, by definition, may return only one instance, such results would be improper. Permitting improper functions can be useful but causes mathematical difficulties. However, multivalued results are highly useful in query operations. In order to preserve the purity of proper functions, yet support multivalued queries, a small adjustment must be made to our foundation. What we must do is permit a function to return multiple instances in the range, yet ensure that the function is proper. One way to achieve this is by using power sets.

> The *power set* of S is the set of all subsets of S, and is written as $\wp(S)$.

Therefore when mapping to a domain, map to the power set of the domain—instead of mapping to just the set. A multivalued function assigns to every element x of a set X to a unique element y in the power set on Y. This is written f:$X \rightarrow \wp(Y)$, where f denotes the function and $\wp(Y)$ the range. It can be stated another way, f(x) = y where y $\in \wp(Y)$. The employer function, above, can be restated as follows:

employer: Person $\rightarrow \wp$(Company)

Function Inverses versus Reverses

In the example above, the employment association was traversed in one direction using the employer function. Evaluating the employee function in the opposite direction is another situation. For example, given a Company object, the employee function returns a single set of Person instances. In other words, employee: Company $\rightarrow \wp$(Person) or, in its more general form, f': $Y \rightarrow \wp(X)$, where f: $X \rightarrow \wp(Y)$. This would be considered the reverse, or adjoint, of the employer function—not the inverse.

The inverse function would—in contrast—take the result of the employer function and return the value that the employer function began with. For instance, f(Bob) = {NASA, IBM}. The inverse, f^{-1}, would begin with the set {NASA, IBM} in its domain and return Bob. Since the range of the inverse may also be multivalued, a more general form for this situation would be where the power type of the domain maps to the power type in the range, or

f^{-1}: $\wp(Y) \rightarrow \wp(X)$.

In summary, to support a 2-place relation in terms of function, a function is paired with another function: either its adjoint or inverse—depending on the user's requirements. The adjoint function provides a function that maps from the set in the range of the original function f; the inverse maps from the power set.

> For each 2-place relation, there is an associated function and either its adjoint or inverse function.*

ATTRIBUTES, ROLES, AND INVARIANTS

Attributes and Roles

Most system developers will model functions as attributes or "role" names on relations. Attributes and role names, then, are presentation techniques for expressing a function. Some developers differentiate solely for graphic clarity: using roles for the "more important" functions and attributes for the less important functions. Such a technique reduces the graphic "noise" on a diagram. Some developers define attributes to be those functions that map to data types (for example, Integer, String, and Real Number); where all other kinds of functions are represented as role names on relations. Other developers expand on this to include complex data types such as Name, Address, Time, and Money. In any case, all are based on a deeper notion—the function.

Invariants

Invariants are Boolean functions over one or more object types and relations that must be true at all times. (Invariants are also known as constraints and rules.) For example, the invariant that a person must always have no more than one employer can be expressed as:

$\forall p \in$ Person: $\mid$ employer (p) $\mid$ ≤ 1.

In this way, the formalisms that have been presented thus far can be employed to constrain the object types and relations. It provides a richer semantic model that expresses business requirements more accurately. Traditional structural definitions alone cannot support this.

---

* The *n*-place relations have *n* associated functions and *n* reverse or inverse functions.

CONCLUSION

While there are many books on OO analysis, few formalize their underlying notions. For most practitioners, this is not a problem. However, building meta-CASE tools, defining repository structures, and comparing OO notations require an exacting approach. Everything must be clear and unambiguous. This article is an initial attempt to produce such a formalism for those structural notions used to represent the results of OO analysis. It presents a basic ontology for expressing our concepts and their relationships using set theory and functions. In short, it defines the essential foundation for meta-modeling or repository-building activities.

REFERENCES

Gray, Peter M. D., *Logic, Algebra, and Databases,* John Wiley and Sons, New York, 1984.

Langer, Susanne K., *An Introduction to Symbolic Logic,* (3rd edition), Dover Publications, New York, 1967.

Martin, James, and James J. Odell, *Object-Oriented Methods: A Foundation,* Prentice-Hall, Englewood Cliffs, NJ, 1996.

Martin, James, and James J. Odell, *Object-Oriented Methods: Pragmatic Considerations,* Prentice-Hall, Englewood Cliffs, NJ, 1996.

Ramackers, Guus, *Integrated Object Modelling,* Thesis Publishers, Amsterdam, 1994.

Russell, Bertrand, *Principles of Mathematics,* Norton, New York, 1938.

Whitehead, Alfred North, and Bertrand Russell, *Principia Mathematica,* Cambridge University Press, Cambridge, 1910.

Part II
Dynamic Issues

O bject dynamics involve the ways in which objects change state. The traditional view of state includes only the data member or attributes of an object. Furthermore, most object languages are restrictive of the objects they create: they may not change classes or be an instance of multiple (non-inheriting) classes. While both of these traditional views are accepted by the OO programming world, they present limitations to the way people think about their world. Again, we have the dichotomy between analysis and design. *What is Object State?* and *Dynamic and Multiple Classification* explore these issues.

Change in state is also a fundamental issue for OO developers. However, not all state changes require us to perform some action. Those state changes that *do* require a response on our part are especially noteworthy. Such state changes are known as events. In *Events and their Specification,* this specialized form of state change is discussed.

This section concludes with a survey of the various ways in which developers represent states and their changes. For example, *Approaches to Finite-State Machine Modeling* compares the Mealy, Moore, and combined Mealy/Moore forms of state-transition modeling.

What is Object State?

May 1992

In object-oriented vocabulary, *state* has particular prominence. OO prac-titioners talk about the state of an object and the changes in state of an object. Yet, people often banter the word about without understanding what state really means. Here, I will explore two common definitions of state. Even though these two definitions are different, they are equivalent. In other words, they are different ways of describing the same phenomenon.

SEQUENCES OF STATE CHANGES OVER TIME

The expression, an object changes, means that the state of an object changes. One common technique for expressing object-state change is a state-tran-sition *fence* diagram depicted in Fig. 6.1a. In this figure, an Airline Reservation object can be in one of several states: Requested, Waitlisted, Denied, and so on. The same Airline Reservation object can also be in a number of other states, such as Unpaid, Deposit Paid, and Fully Paid (Fig. 6.1b). Taking both dia-grams into account, the same Airline Reservation object can be Waitlisted *and* Deposit Paid, Cancelled *and* Needs Refund, or various other combinations.

Within each state-transition diagram, an object is only allowed to be in one state at a time. In this way, the OO developer can concentrate on a particular facet of an object's *lifecycle*. However, as we see in the example above, the state of most objects is richer than one diagram can or should try to express. To describe the *complete* state of an object, multiple state-tran-sition diagrams are often used. For instance, the process of the Jane object leaving her job (in Fig. 6.2) involved a reasonably complex change: she went from being a Manager, IBM Employee, Company Employee, Person, Brown-haired, and Pet Owner to being a Nonemployee, a Person, Brown-

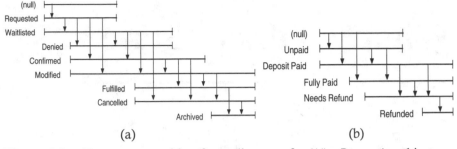

Figure 6.1.   Two state-transition fence diagrams for Airline Reservation objects.

haired, and a Pet Owner.* Such state components and their changes could be described in several state-transition diagrams. One diagram could specify employment-related state transitions, another could specify those state transitions dealing with owning animals, and one more could specify those state transitions that only her hairdresser should know. However, the complete understanding of Jane's state comes from taking all of these diagrams together.

Despite the fact that we use states to describe objects at various moments in time, the questions still remain: What is state? How does it relate to object-oriented specification?

STATE AS A COLLECTION OF ASSOCIATIONS OF AN OBJECT

When implemented by an OO programming language, object state is recorded in the data stored about the object. It is defined by the classes and attribute values associated with an object. Therefore, one definition of state commonly used by OO programmers is as follows:

> The *state* of an object is the collection of associations that an object has.

---

* Yes, Pet Owners can be objects other than Person objects. For example, both Jane and the Evanston Emus Drum and Bugle Corps can have Emus as pets. Similarly, objects in a Brown-haired state are not confined to being persons.

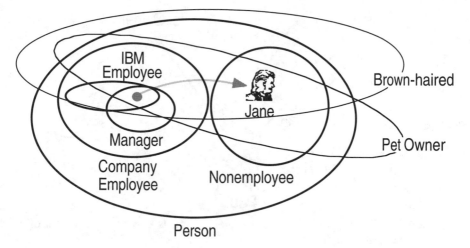

Figure 6.2.   A complex state transition of a Person object.

An object named Paul (in Fig. 6.3) is expressed in terms of its associations with other objects. Paul's current state, then, is a collection of four associations indicating that Paul is employed by NASA, has red hair, and is classified as both a Pet Owner and a Person. If Paul becomes unemployed, changes his hair color, no longer owns pets, and so on, Paul's state will change. His state will change, because his collection of associations will have changed.

From Fig. 6.3, we can immediately see that the Paul object is an instance of at least two object types (or classes): Pet Owner and Person. We know this because every object type *classifies* objects, and objects are *classified as* (or instances of) object types. For example in Fig. 6.4, a set of objects is classified as Person objects. In other words, the object named Person (which is an instance of Object Type) has an association that *classifies* the objects Susan, Jane, Paul, and so on. The classifies association, then, is just another association among many others, such as employs. The only thing special about the classifies association is that most OO languages implement classification by mapping a class to its objects. However, other associations are typically implemented as instance variables (or fields) that map objects to other objects. However, when classes are thought of as objects in their own right, *all* associations map objects to other objects. (In this way, the set of Object Types in Fig. 6.4 is really a subset of Objects as well, that is, Object Type is a subtype of Object.)

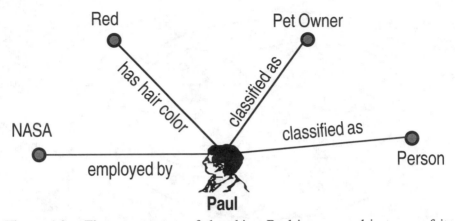

Figure 6.3. The current state of the object Paul is expressed in terms of its associations with other objects.

A different kind of association is depicted in Fig. 6.5. Here, objects that are *not* object types map to a set of objects. For instance, the NASA object maps to a set containing objects Paul and Jasper, NEC maps to a set containing Susan, PanAm maps to an empty set, and so on. As with the example in Fig. 6.4, mapping from a given object determines a set of other objects. In this case, instances of Object Type are not mapped to sets of objects: Organization objects are mapped to sets of Person objects. While both are associations that an object has, one is classification related and the other employment related.

THE SEGUE: OBJECT TYPES VERSUS OBJECT ASSOCIATIONS

In OO analysis, I use the term object type and concept synonymously. An object type, therefore, is an idea or notion that we apply to certain objects in our awareness. So, thinking of the Person and Pet Owner states as object types is quite natural. To say that you have the concept, or object type, of Person and Pet Owner only requires the ability to identify an actual person or pet owner.

Furthermore, each object type is a concept—each has an extension and an intension. The extension of an object type is the set of objects to which the object type applies. The intension is the complete object-type definition. The extension of Person in Fig. 6.4 is the set of objects to which Person applies: Susan, Jane, Jasper, Paul, and so on. The intension of Person is the

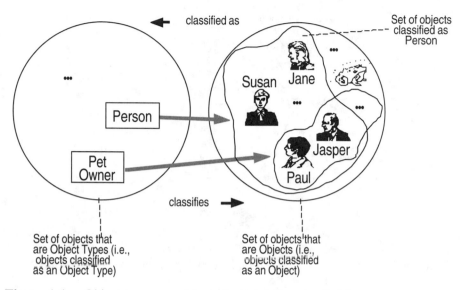

Figure 6.4.   Object types are objects that classify sets of objects.

complete definition of what it means for an object to be classified as a human being.

The same idea can be used for the object associations in Fig. 6.5. For example, can the mapping of NASA to its employees constitute an object type? Here, the extension of the NASA employs mapping is the set containing the objects Jasper and Paul. The intension is defined simply in terms of whether or not an object is one that NASA employs. In other words, here is an idea or notion that applies to certain objects. Additionally, this *idea* has both an extension and intension. If this is so, what should the object type be called that is based on NASA's employs mapping? In Fig. 6.6, it is simply named NASA Employee. NASA Employee, then, applies to those Person objects that are employed by NASA—*because* those objects are associated with NASA via the employs mapping. Similarly, the object type named Red-haired Object applies to those objects that have a hair color attribute of Red.

This is no slight of hand but two sides of the same coin. For instance, what is the difference between these two statements?

- I want to refer to those Person objects that are associates with the NASA Organization via its employs mapping.
- I want to refer to NASA Employee objects.

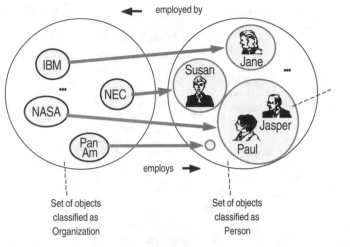

Figure 6.5.   Objects of the Organization type map to sets of the Person type.

Actually, these two statements simply describe the same notion in two different ways, they are equivalent in meaning. When the first statement is made, the second can be automatically inferred.

STATE AS A COLLECTION OF OBJECT TYPES

Figure 6.6 illustrates the various sets of objects to which four object types apply: Person, Pet Owner, NASA Employee, and Red-haired Object. In other words, the state of the Paul object introduced in Fig. 6.3 is now defined in terms of a collection of object types that applies to it. An alternate, yet equivalent, definition of state is as follows:

> The *state* of an object is the collection of object types that applies to it.

CONCLUSION

I have tried to clear up some of the confusion about object state. Some OO practitioners prefer to define the state of an object as a collection of associations for that object. Others prefer to define it as a collection of object types—of which the object is an instance. The point is that both

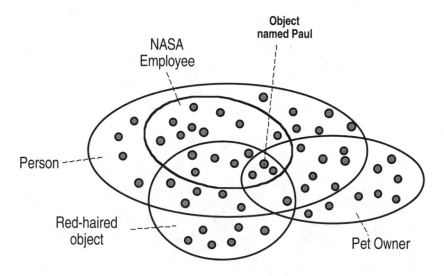

Figure 6.6. Paul is an object that is an instance of four object types.

are correct. They are just two ways of describing the *same* phenomenon. The eclectic analyst, then, will not choose only one or the other. Both are ways of describing the existence of an object—whether from an object-type standpoint or an object-association standpoint. In OO analysis, the decision of which to use should be based on clarity and ease of communication with people.

Dynamic and Multiple Classification

January 1992

Object-oriented analysis should *not* model reality—rather it should model the way reality is understood by *people*. The understanding and knowledge of people is the essential component in developing systems. Therefore, OO analysis should not be based on any implementation technology—including OO software implementation. As Brad Cox [Cox, 1990] so eloquently expressed it, "'object-oriented' refers to the war, not the weapons. . . ." When practiced in this way, OO analysis allows us to analyze *any* area of human reality—not *just* that of data processing. In addition, this allows us to implement our conceptual model using technologies other than OO programming languages (OOPLs).

The approach to design, however, is different. As illustrated in Fig. 7.1, design is defined as a process that specifies how the conceptual model of analysis will be implemented. A shift in thinking must take place from defining *what* is needed to *how* it can be provided. One of the reasons why the OO approach has been so successful is because the shift from concept to implementation is smaller than with conventional approaches. For instance, the *objects* we perceive can be implemented as objects in OO systems. The *types of objects* we define can be implemented as classes in OO systems.

However, the shift from an OO conceptual model to an OO implementation model is not always so smooth. This month's column explores two such areas: dynamic classification and multiple classification.

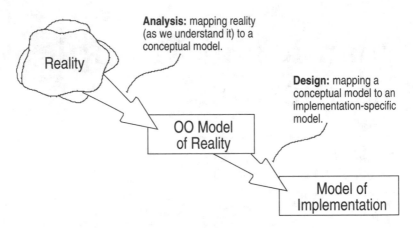

Figure 7.1.   Analysis and design as different mappings.

DYNAMIC CLASSIFICATION

Dynamic classification (also called dynamic typing) refers to the ability to change the classification of an object. For example in Fig. 7.2, the "Alice" object changes from being an instance of Employee, Manager, and Salesperson to being a Unemployed Person. However, she still remains an instance of the object type Person. In other words, with dynamic classification, an object can be an instance of different object types from moment to moment.

Object Life Cycles

When we determine that an object is of a specific type, the object is *classified* as an instance of that object type. When an object is no longer a particular type of object, the object is *declassified* and removed as an instance of that object type. Figure 7.3 portrays the "Alice" object being classified and declassified in terms of the object type Employee. At some point in her life, Alice is first classified as an Employee. Later, through some process, Alice is declassified as an Employee: she becomes unemployed. At another point, Alice may become reemployed, followed again by a period of unemployment. This behavior may continue until retirement is reached or the process of death takes place.

Figure 7.3 illustrates the lifecycle of an "Alice" object in terms of one object type. (Figures 7.2, 7.4, and 7.5 indicate portions of the object's lifecycle in terms of several object types.) Without dynamic classification, the

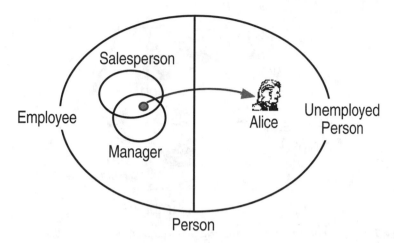

Figure 7.2. Dynamic classification refers to the ability to change an object's type.

classification of the "Alice" object cannot change. Therefore, every time she is removed from the Employee class Alice would cease to exist. To make things worse, when she became reemployed she would be created as a new object—devoid of any already-existing attributes and past history. Dynamic classification, then, permits objects to exist independently of the object types by which they are classified—and allows their termination.*

Implementing Dynamic Classification

Specifying classification changes is an important aspect of OO analysis. However, while Smalltalk, CLOS, and Iris support dynamic classification to a limited extent, the remaining OO programming languages offer no direct support. To implement dynamic classification requires the skill of an OO designer to develop a "work-around" solution. One solution is that whenever an object changes classes, a new object is created. The appropriate properties from the old object are copied to the new object, and the old object is finally terminated.

Another solution is to define a status flag that indicates the classification. For example, the Person class could contain an employment_status field indi-

---

* Note: An object cannot exist without any classification. Therefore, as long as an object is classified by at least one object type, the object still exists. In the case of Alice, Fig. 7.2 indicates that when she is declassified as Employee, Alice would still be an instance of Person. In other words, Alice survives the employment termination process. When an object is finally terminated, it is declassified of all of its object types.

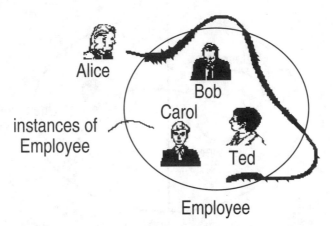

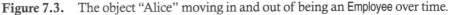

Figure 7.3. The object "Alice" moving in and out of being an Employee over time.

cating whether or not a Person object is employed or not. In this scenario, the programmer would need to write extra code to override method selection. For instance, even though the retire_Employee method would be associated with the Person class, it may not be invoked for unemployed persons. Therefore, the employment_status field would have to be checked first to determine whether or not the person is employed. In other words, a person's employment state would have to be evaluated by customized code instead of the method-selection mechanism inherent in OO software.

The point is no matter which implementation is chosen, the notion that an object can be classified and declassified is foreign to most OO languages.

MULTIPLE CLASSIFICATION

Figure 7.3 depicts an object in terms of only one object type. However, the "Alice" object may be classified and declassified as various object types over time. At the age of eighteen, she will change from the object type Girl to the object type Woman. At some point, she may get married and become an instance of the object types Married Person and Wife. Quite independently, she may be confirmed as a Supreme Court Justice or buy a pet and become a Pet Owner. While she may be a Supreme Court Justice for life, she may later give the pet away and be removed from the Pet Owner set.

In her lifetime, Alice may be an instance of many object types. This means, first, that the object types that apply to an object can change over time (dynamic classification). Second, it means that an object can have multiple object types that apply to it at any one moment. When an object is an instance of more than one object type, this is called multiple classification (not to be confused with multiple inheritance).

Multiple classification is alien to most data-processing implementations. Typically, a data record can only be obtained via its creating record type. Most OO programming languages are similarly restrictive, requiring an object to be an instance of one OOPL class for life—not counting the object's superclasses. However, in OO analysis, we are not modeling how computer languages and databases work, we are analyzing our enterprise world as *people* would see it.

The class/subclass hierarchy is one way of classifying an object in multiple ways. For example, if Alice is an instance of the Employee class, she is also an instance of Person (Fig. 7.4). In other words, when Alice is classified as an Employee, the Person classification is implied by the superclass hierarchy.

However, an object can also be an instance of multiple classes that are not implied from a superclass hierarchy. For example, multiple classification makes it possible for the "Alice" object to be an instance of both the Employee and Pet Owner classes. Since the Pet Owner class is not a superclass of Employee, being an Employee does not automatically imply being a Pet Owner. Therefore, if Alice is an instance of Employee, she is not necessarily an instance of Pet Owner—and vice versa. In order for Alice to be both a Pet Owner and an Employee, Alice must be explicitly classified as both. Over time, this change in classification could look something like the graph in Fig. 7.5.

Implementing Multiple Classification

Multiple classification, based on a class/subclass hierarchy, is supported and is one of the benefits of OOPLs. However, multiple classifications that

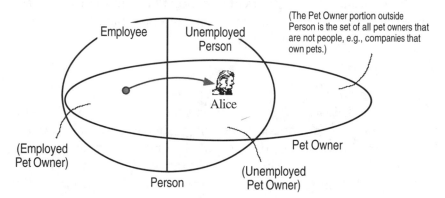

Figure 7.4. The object "Alice" involved in both dynamic classification and multiple classification.

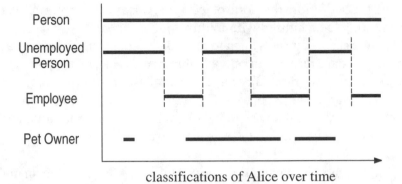

classifications of Alice over time

Figure 7.5. In the "real world," not only can the classifications of an object change, the object can be an instance of several object types at the same moment.

are *not* part of an object's inheritance hierarchy are not supported by OOPLs. Typically, if a developer wishes to "get around" this limitation, additional classes are specified. These additional classes define the necessary multiple-classification combinations. For instance, to support the "Alice" object as a Pet Owner that can also be an Employee or an Unemployed Person, two additional subclasses (Fig. 7.6) are defined: Employed Pet Owner and Unemployed Pet Owner. The Unemployed Pet Owner class will be a subclass of both Unemployed Person and Pet Owner; the Employed Pet Owner class will be a subclass of both Employee and Pet Owner. In this way, multiple classification could be handled via the multiple inheritance mechanism supported by some OOPLs. This approach has two drawbacks. First, a class is needed for every multiple-classification combination that can occur within a system (where 2^n combinations are theoretically possible). Second, not all OOPLs support multiple inheritance.

Object Slicing

Another common technique that supports multiple (as well as dynamic) classification is called *object slicing*. In object slicing, an object with multiple classifications can be thought of as being "sliced" into multiple pieces. Each piece is then distributed to one of the object's various classes. For example in Fig. 7.5, the "Alice" object is depicted as an instance of the Employee and Pet Owner classes. To implement these two facts in an OOPL, one piece of the "Alice" object must become an instance of Employee and the other an instance of Pet Owner.

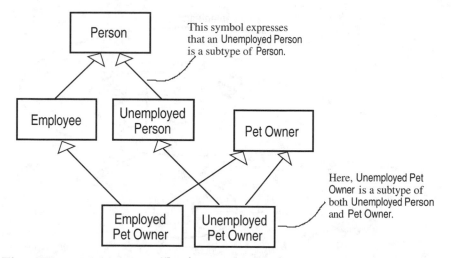

Figure 7.6.   Multiple classification can be implemented via a multiple inheritance mechanism. In this diagram, Employee, Unemployed Person, and Pet Owner are classes whose combinations define the subclasses Employed Pet Owner and Unemployed Pet Owner.

Obviously, objects cannot be "sliced" and made into instances of classes: it is a metaphor. These "slices," however, can be implemented by surrogate objects. In addition, an "unsliced" version of the object must also be recorded to serve—physically and conceptually—as a unification point for its surrogates. The slices, then, become the various recorded aspects of one unsliced object. One way to accomplish this is by adding two new classes: Implementation Object and Conceptual Object. The instances of Implementation Object are the object slices, where each is an instance of a different class. The instances of Conceptual Object are the unsliced objects, where each maintains pointers to its various slices.

An example of how object slicing can be applied is illustrated in Fig. 7.7. In this figure, the unsliced "Alice" object is represented as an instance of the Conceptual Object class. This one object representing "Alice" as a whole points to multiple "Alice" object slices. Since these slices represent different class implementations of the conceptual "Alice" object, they are instances of the Implementation Object class. The instances in the Pet Owner and Employee classes are slices of the "Alice" object. In other words, object slices of the whole "Alice" object are also "Alice" objects. However, the slices comply with the conventional OOPL requirement that each is an instance of only one class.

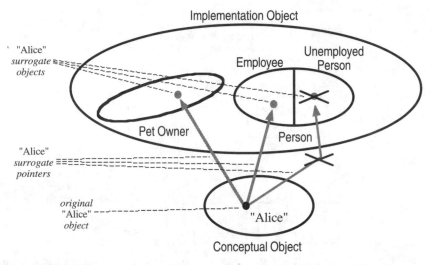

Figure 7.7.   Object slicing supports dynamic and multiple classification.

Additionally, changes in state can be accomplished by adding or removing the surrogates and the pointers to them. For instance, when Alice was classified as Unemployed Person, there was a pointer from the Conceptual Object "Alice" to the Unemployed Person "Alice" surrogate. When Alice became employed, the surrogate Unemployed Person object and its pointer were removed and replaced by a surrogate Employee "Alice" object and its pointer.

As each object is added or removed from the various classes, the construction and destruction operations of those classes would still apply. However, the object-slicing mechanism must add to these class-level operations by ensuring that objects do not have conflicting multiple states. For example, an object can simultaneously be an instance of the Pet Owner and Employee classes. However, it cannot simultaneously be an instance of both the Unemployed Person and Employee classes. For an object to be classified as an Unemployed Person, the object must be removed as an instance of the Employee class.

Object slicing is a reasonably elegant solution to a problem not yet directly supported by OOPLs. However, in addition to the programming overhead mentioned above, object slicing also requires extra logic to support polymorphism and supplement the OOPL's method-selection mechanism.

CONCLUSION

This column examined two important modeling phenomena:

* dynamic classification.
* multiple classification.

In analysis, they provide very useful notions that describe some of the ways we think about our world. The transition to OO implementation, however, is not a smooth one. While "work-around" solutions are possible, OO programming languages provide little or no *direct* support for these notions. If it were a voting issue, I would certainly cast mine in favor of enhancing OO programming languages so that these notions are directly supported. (In fact, I would like to hear how some of you might vote.) In the meantime, the OO designer will have more work to do.

REFERENCES

Cox, Brad J., "Planning the Software Industrial Revolution," *IEEE Software,* 7:6, November 1990, pp. 25–33.

Events and their Specification

July/August 1994

In astronomy or physics, changes in state are common occurrences—a star explodes, a comet's orbit changes, a radioactive particle decays. Most of these state changes are unnoticed or undetectable by us. However, if we wish to know about and react to them in some way, their occurrence must be noted. Events, then, serve as markers for the points in time when state changes occur.

Without events, the world as we know it would not change. In such a world, we could build and populate databases without concern for updating them. However in most applications, database contents do change. To react appropriately to such changes, we need to understand and model events. This column elaborates on the nature of events and describes how to specify their state changes and focuses on

- What is the difference between a state change and an event?
- What does it mean that, fundamentally, there are only two kinds of state changes—add and remove?
- How can we extend this to include changes in which objects are created, terminated, classified, declassified, connected, and disconnected?

EVENTS VERSUS STATE CHANGES

Our world is full of changes. Aunt Betty arrives unexpectedly. An airline booking is canceled. A machine tool breaks down. A job is completed.

Such changes in state are important to us, because they signal a need to acknowledge the change in some way. For instance in Fig. 8.1, the traffic light can change between three basic states. If we are distant from this traffic light, its changes are unknown and, therefore, unimportant to us. However, if we arrive at the intersection when it changes to yellow or red, we should react appropriately. When state changes are important enough for us to acknowledge, they are called *events*.

An *event* is a noteworthy change in state.

BASIC EVENTS

Fundamentally, two kinds of state changes occur: add and remove. An *add* state change brings a new object or relationship into existence. A *remove* state change removes an object or relationship from existence. For example. the person labeled Paul in Fig. 8.2 decided to leave NASA and form his own company called HAL Explorations. Here, a state change is required to remove not NASA or Paul, but to remove Paul's employment relationship with NASA.* Another state change is required to add a new Company object named HAL Explorations. Yet another state change is required to add a new employment relationship between Paul and HAL Explorations.

While state changes *fundamentally* add and remove objects, specifying changes in this way is not always user friendly. For instance, when Paul buys his first pet, a state change would add an association between Paul and the Pet Owner object type. While such a statement is technically correct, perhaps it would be clearer to say that the state change *classifies* Paul as a Pet Owner. However, specifying the addition of employed by or has hair color associations in this way would not be appropriate. Instead, we could say that the HAL Explorations and Paul objects are *connected* in a new relationship, and the old NASA and Paul relationship is *disconnected*. These and other specifications are addressed with several basic kinds of state changes. In particular, this column discusses how objects can be created, terminated, classified, declassified, reclassified, connected, disconnected, coalesced,

---

* Relationships can be treated as objects in their own right. Here, the employment relationship between NASA and Paul is an instance of a relationship *type* between Organizations and Persons.

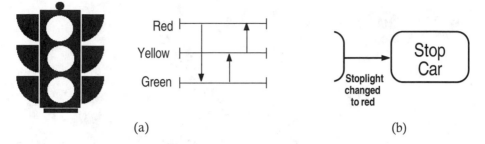

(a)   (b)

Figure 8.1. The traffic light in (a) can change state in three ways. State changes that we should acknowledge are *events*—such as a stoplight changing to red as we approach an intersection (b).

and decoalesced. Every event can be classified as one of these kinds of state changes—even though each fundamentally involves adding or removing objects.

Creation Event

In a *creation* event, an entirely new object appears. For example, the event type Breakfast started occurs when an object is created and becomes a member of the Breakfast set in Fig. 8.3(a). Order received indicates that an object is created as an instance of the object type Order. An object cannot exist without being an instance of at least one object type. Therefore, each time an object is created, it must become a member of at least one object type's set. In this way, a creation event is the change from not being an object at all to that of being an object of at least one specific type. In a *termination* event, an existing object is removed from our awareness. For example in Fig. 8.3(b), the event type Breakfast completed occurs when a Breakfast object no longer exists. Order terminated indicates that an instance of Order is terminated from existence.

The state change is from the state of being an object of one or more types to not being an object at all. For example, the Breakfast object in Fig. 8.3(b) may have been an instance of Artform and Food Fight Object as well. However after termination, the object is no longer an instance of any object type. As long as even one object type applies, the object still exists in some way. When no object types apply, the object cannot exist.

Classification Event

A *classification* event is the classification of an *existing* object. For example in Fig. 8.4(a), the event type Person classified Employee occurs when a Person

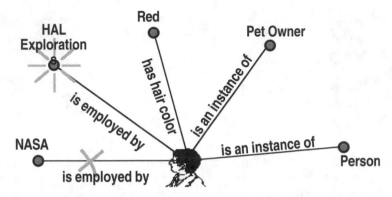

Figure 8.2.   State changes result in adding or removing objects. Since relationships can also be treated as objects, state changes can add and remove them as well.

object *also* becomes a member of the Employee set. Order shipped occurs when an Order object is also classified as an instance of Shipped Order. In this state change, an object becomes a member of a set of which it was not previously a member. In other words, a specific set is extended by one previously existing object.

Declassification Event

A *declassification* event is the declassification of an existing object. In Fig. 8.4(b), the event type Person declassified Employee occurs when a Person object is removed as a member of the Employee set—after which the object remains a Person but is no longer an Employee. Account declassified Overdue Account indicates that the Overdue Account object type no longer applies to a specific Account object. The state change is from being an object of one or more sets to that of being an object of one less set. (A declassification event that results in no object types applying to a particular object is equivalent to a termination event.)

Connection Event

A *connection* event adds an entirely new relationship between two objects. For example in Fig. 8.5(a), the event type Person employed occurs when a Person object is associated to an Organization via an is employed by/employs relationship. Order Shipping Date assigned occurs when a Shipping Date property is established for a particular Order. Such an event appears to be the same as a *create* event, because a new object—albeit, a *relationship* object, or tuple— is created. While this is true, some developers prefer the metaphor of

Breakfast

(a)

Breakfast

(b)

Figure 8.3. Object creation and termination.

connecting objects an easier one to understand. Connection events, then, are creation events for relationships. The state change is the change from not being a relationship at all to that of being a relationship of some particular type.

Disconnection Event

A *disconnection* event removes an existing relationship between two objects. For example in Fig. 8.5(b), the event type Person unemployed occurs when an is employed by/employs relationship is removed between a Person object and an Organization object. Disconnection events, then, are termination events for relationships. The state change is from being a relationship of some type to being a relationship that no longer exists.

COMPOUND EVENTS

Create, terminate, classify, declassify, connect, disconnect are the kinds of events that either add or remove an object from a set. However, some events are more transactional, because they require simultaneous adds and removes. This is particularly true of reclassification and reconnection events.

Reclassification Event

A *reclassification* event is the simultaneous declassification of an object as one object type and classification of it as another object type. In Fig. 8.6(a), a marriage event type occurs when an object is removed from the Unmarried Person set and is added to the set Married Person. The state change was from the state of being an object in one set, to that of being an object in a different set. Put another way, one specific set is reduced by one object and another specific set is extended by same object—simultaneously.

Figure 8.4.   Object classification and declassification.

Object reclassification is a compound event, because it consists of an object-declassification event and an object-classification event. It is useful when these two events cannot occur separately. For example, a Person object must either be married or unmarried. Declassifying an Unmarried Person object without *simultaneously* classifying it as a Married Person would create an illogical void. Object reclassification eliminates the difficulties of this by classifying and declassifying at the same time. This is particularly useful for reclassifying an object between subtypes that are within the same partition.

Reconnection Event

A *reconnection* event is the simultaneous termination of one relationship and creation of another of the same type—while keeping one of its related objects the same throughout. For example, in Fig. 8.6(b) each relationship, or tuple, in a Residence Location relationship associates a Person object and a Location object. Adding a relationship, then, is a connection event; removing a relationship is a disconnection event. However, due to cardinality constraints, a particular type of relationship may be required at all times. For instance, assume that the Residence Location relationship type requires that each Person object relate to *exactly* one Location object at all times. To remove a relationship—even for a moment—violates the Residence Location cardinality constraint. Such a situation makes changing a person's residence impossible unless Residence Location relationships can be

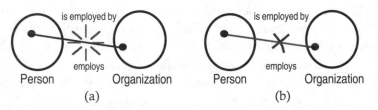

Figure 8.5.   Object connection and disconnection.

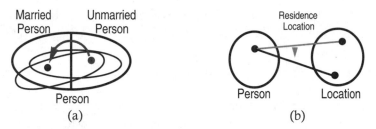

Figure 8.6.   Reclassification and reconnection events.

terminated and created simultaneously. The reconnection event eliminates the difficulties of this by connecting and disconnecting at the same time. This is particularly useful for those mappings whose minimum cardinality is one (that is, mandatory).

Other Compound Events

Reclassification and reconnection are two common, compound event types. In addition to these, many analysts suggest the need for others, the most popular of which are component termination, coalesce, and decoalesce.

 Component termination is an event indicating that not only an object is terminated, but all of its components are as well. For example, the component termination of a Boat object means that when the Boat object is terminated, its Hull and Motor component objects are terminated at the same time. Component termination is appropriate only when the components of an object are terminated along with the object itself. If they are not, component termination is inappropriate. For instance, if a Motor object survives the termination of its Boat, component termination is not applicable here—only object termination.

 In a *coalesce* event, a set of objects—previously recognized as distinct— becomes the same object. For example, many mystery stories have one Murderer object and a Butler object. Following the event called The Butler did It, these two objects are perceived as one and the same object. As indicated in Fig. 8.7(a), all object types that applied to each object separately now apply

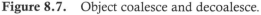

Figure 8.7.   Object coalesce and decoalesce.

to the coalesced object. The previous two objects are henceforth recognized as the same thing. The *object decoalesce* in Fig. 8.7(b) has the opposite effect.

EVENT PRESTATES AND POSTSTATES

As indicated earlier, each event is a change in the state of one object. This change implies that each event has a specified prestate and a specified poststate.

> An *event prestate* is a state that *must* apply to an object *before* the event occurs.
>
> An *event poststate* is a state that *must* apply to an object *after* the event occurs.

Figure 8.8(a) specifies the prestates and poststates required for each of the eight most common kinds of events. In addition, Fig. 8.8(b) provides examples of each of these kinds of events.

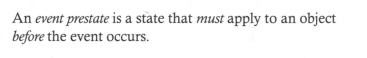

event type	event prestate	event poststate
X created	not Object	X
X terminated	X	not Object
X classified C	X, but not C	X and C
X declassified C	X and C	X, but not C
R connected	No R between C1 and C2 objects	R between C1 and C2 objects
R disconnected	R between C1 and C2 objects	No R between C1 and C2 objects
X reclassified from C1 to C2	X and C1, but not C2	X and C2, but not C1
R reconnected from C1 to C2	R1 but no R2 between C1 and C2 objects	R2 but no R1 between C1 and C2 objects

(a)

Event Example	event prestate	event poststate
Breakfast created	not Object	Breakfast
Breakfast terminated	Breakfast	not Object
Person classified Employee	Person, but not Employee	Person and Employee
Person declassified Employee	Person and Employee	Person, but not Employee
Person employed	Organization and Person not related	Organization and Person related
Person unemployed	Organization and Person related	Organization and Person not related
Person married	Unmarried Person	Married Person
Residence changed	Residence	Residence (different tuple)

(b)

Figure 8.8.   Examples of event prestates and poststates for the eight most common kinds of events.

Approaches to Finite-State Machine Modeling

January 1995

Finite-state machines (FSMs) are a popular form for representing OO behavior, because FSMs can be readily mapped to OO programming languages. In an OO programming language, each FSM can be implemented with a class. Each FSM operation, then, is naturally associated with the class that implements the FSM. With such a straightforward mapping, it is no wonder that several OO methodologies employ FSM-based representation. This article explores the following:

- How is OO behavior expressed using FSM-based representation?
- When should FSM-based representations be used and not used?
- How can FSM-based representations be summarized?
- Can FSM-based representations be used with other kinds of representations?

VARIETIES OF FSM

FSM representations differ principally in where operations are expressed. When the operation is associated with the transition, the representation is known as the *Mealy model* of FSMs. When the operation is associated with the state, it is known as the *Moore model* of FSMs. Operations associated with both the state *and* the transition are called the *Mealy/Moore combination model*.

In his first book [Booch, 1991], Grady Booch employed the Mealy model. The representation used in this book is called the *state-transition diagram* and is illustrated in Fig. 9.1. This diagram specifies a FSM for an Action object. For instance, the starting state is when the Action is Proposed. From this state, an Action can be Initiated, Abandoned, Suspended, or Completed. If an Action started event occurs, the Create Implemented Action operation is invoked—resulting in the Action being classified as Initiated.

One of the perceived drawbacks of the original Mealy approach is that it does not support the notion of conditional transitions. For instance in Fig. 9.1, an Action resumed event can occur for a Suspended Action. However, given this event and state, it is unclear which operation should be invoked—Resume Implementation or Resume Proposal. With the ability to specify operations on states, the Moore model can express which transition should occur under which circumstances. Figure 9.2 depicts a *state-model* diagram from the Shlaer approach [Shlaer, 1992]. Here, the state named *Action Resuming* has a Lift Suspension operation whose method is expressed in a language-based approach. This method chooses which operation should be invoked based on whether or not the Action has already been in an Action Initiated state. If the Action were in an Action Initiated state, the Resume Implementation operation would be invoked. Otherwise, the Resume Proposal operation would be invoked.

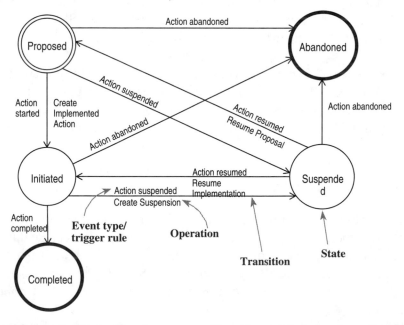

Figure 9.1. A Grady Booch *state-transition diagram* that employs the *Mealy model* of FSMs.

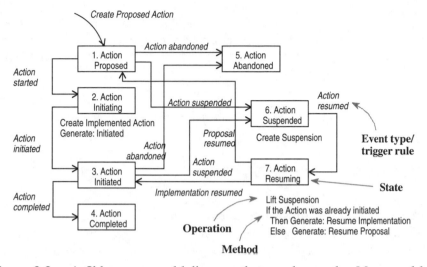

Figure 9.2. A Shlaer *state-model* diagram that employees the *Moore model* of FSMs.

The Moore modeling approach is also perceived to have drawbacks. For instance, the FSM in Fig. 9.2 required two more states that the FSM in Fig. 9.1—Action Resuming and Action Initiating. Furthermore, the ability to specify operations on transitions is not permitted. The current trend is to employ a combination of Mealy and Moore modeling techniques. In this way, the analyst can get the best of both techniques. Figure 9.3 illustrates the representation syntax for the three OO-FSM approaches by Booch [Booch, 1994], Embley [Embley, 1992], and Rumbaugh [Rumbaugh, 1991]. For states, these three can express operations and their methods within the state symbol. Additionally, operations can be specified on transitions—along with the event/trigger and control (or *guard*) condition specifications.

Another level of sophistication for FSMs is described by David Harel [Harel, 1988] and has subsequently been taken up by Booch and Rumbaugh. The most notable extension is the notion of superstates and substates. Superstates and substates are based on the generalization of object states. An example of a Booch and Rumbaugh state-transition diagram with superstates and substates is illustrated in Fig. 9.4. In this example, the Proposed and Initiated states are substates of the Active state. In other words, every object that is in a Proposed or Initiated state is—by implication—also in an Active state. The Active state, then, is a superstate that can be partitioned as a Proposed state or an Initiated state.

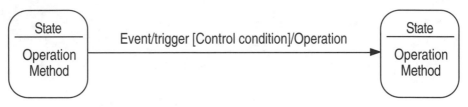

Figure 9.3.   The FSM representation used by Booch, Embley, and Rumbaugh employs a combination of Mealy and Moore.

BEHAVIOR BETWEEN TYPES

The FSM diagrams illustrated above provide one way of representing behavior. The behavior of several FSMs can be diagrammed on one piece of paper. However, *many* FSM diagrams on the same page would be overwhelming. A picture can be worth a thousand words, but a picture *with* a thousand words is something else. Therefore, a different representation technique is required.

Object-Type Interaction Diagram

One commonly used technique is the *object-type interaction* diagram. Instead of displaying each FSM in detail, only the FSM object types are depicted. A simple stock-delivery application, for example, could be specified with several FSM diagrams. However, indicating the way these various FSM diagrams interact could be too complex visually. To reduce this complexity, just the appropriate object types could be represented along with the necessary inter-FSM requests. Figure 9.5 illustrates one way of visualizing inter-FSM behavior. This diagram employs the Booch notation.

Again, diagrams such as the one illustrated in Fig. 9.5 help us to visualize inter-FSM behavior. However, diagramming the *sequence* of the behavior is a different problem. Some approaches indicate the sequence with numbers on the transition lines. For example, Fig. 9.6 uses the Coad technique to indicate the sequence in which operations should occur to pay an employee.

Notation such as this is useful as long as the sequence is simple and linear and each object type has no more than one operation depicted. When the sequence involves many invocations among many object types and operations, the diagram quickly becomes too complex. Expressing concurrent invocation, looping, and condition testing adds yet another level of complexity. To cope with these more complex requirements, other speci-

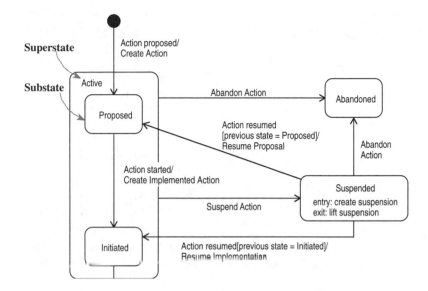

Figure 9.4.   An example of a state-transition diagram with superstates and sub-states as represented by Booch and Rumbaugh.

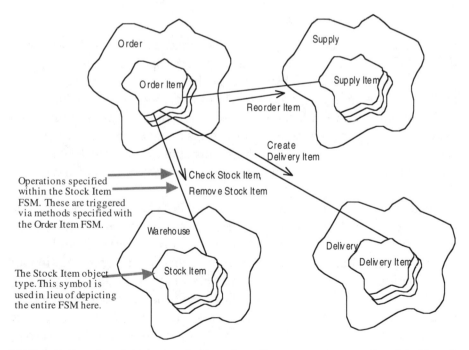

Figure 9.5.   An object-type interaction diagram represented using Booch notation.

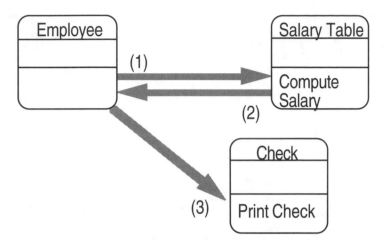

Figure 9.6.   An example using Coad notation that indicates the sequence in which operations should occur to pay an employee.

fication approaches should be explored. The scenario-based specification is one such technique.

Finite State versus Scenario Approaches

Each finite-state machine specifies state changes and operations for a particular type of object. In contrast, scenario-based specifications can involve many object types at once. They express behavior as a *series* of state changes and operations in the script-like form. In other words, object states and their state changes are still expressed—just in a different graphic form. An example of a scenario-based specification is depicted in Fig. 9.7 using an activity diagram. The same order-processing application could be expressed in a FSM-based form. The four state-transition diagrams depicted in Fig. 9.8 are such an example.

Furthermore, the analyst does not have to choose just one specification technique. Since FSM- and scenario-based representations are state related, the segue from one kind of representation to another is relatively straightforward. In this way, the analyst can choose one representation for one situation and a different representation for another. For example, Fig. 9.9 depicts a simplified FSM form called a *fence diagram*. To the right of the fence diagram is an activity diagram. This activity diagram expresses the method for the Dressed to Primed transition. Figure 9.10 indicates how a particular event in an activity diagram relates to the corresponding state change in a fence diagram. In this way, the analyst is not restricted to

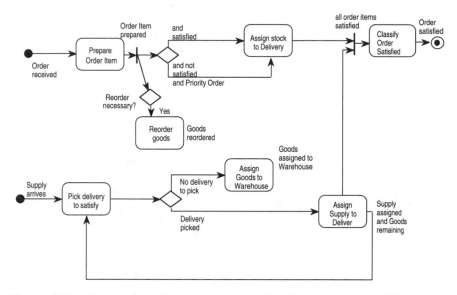

Figure 9.7. A sample order-processing application expressed with scenario-based representation called an *activity diagram.*

choosing only one kind of notation. For problems best described by a FSM, a state-transition diagram could be used. For problems best descibed with a script-like structure, scenarios could be used.

WHEN TO USE OR AVOID FSM-BASED REPRESENTATION

FSM-based representations are often found useful in the following situations:

- *When a particular kind of object has a complex behavior.* For example, elevators, vending machines, and digital alarm clocks are good candidates for FSMs. Each has a type of object that changes state in many ways. Light switches could be in this list, but their on-off behavior is often seen as too simplistic to bother creating a FSM.
- *When a few number of objects interact.* For example, stop lights on a street corner, a control signal and a train, or a pump control system are good candidates for FSMs. In other words, when the state of one object changes, a state change in a second object could be triggered.

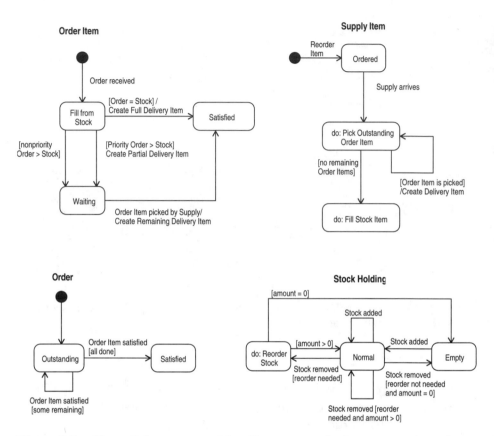

Figure 9.8.   Four of the state-transition diagrams required to support the order-processing activity diagram in Fig. 9.7.

- *When object behavior is event driven and single threaded.* For example, voice-mail systems are driven by events from users entering numbers and symbols on a telephone keypad. The system is single threaded because the transitions from one state to another are serial.
- *When an object is viewed as being in only one state at any given moment.* For example, a library book is usually perceived as being in only one state at a time.
- *When user experts find that FSMs are the best way describe their system.* There are many ways user experts can express the behavior of their system. If a user expert finds that FSMs provide the clearest way of thinking about and representing a particular system requirement, FSMs should be used.

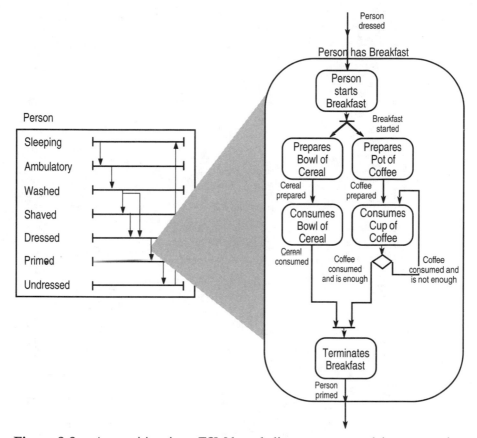

Figure 9.9.   A transition in a FSM-based diagram expressed in a scenario-based notation.

FSMs provide a useful expression of object behavior under several circumstances. However, this does not mean that FSMs should *always* be used. For example, FSMs should probably not be used in the following circumstances:

- *When an object is viewed as being in many states at any given moment.* A Person object can be an infant, child, adolescent, or adult. The same object can be employed or unemployed, a homeowner or not, a pet owner or not, a parent or not, creditworthy or not, and so on. Each of these categories is a different aspect of one particular object's state. To model the *complete* state of an object, a FSM could be defined with all possible combinations. Another option would

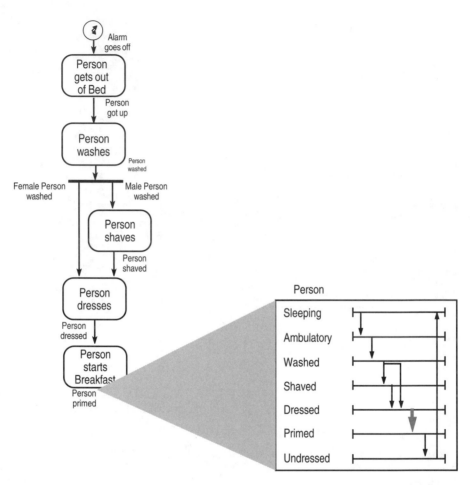

Figure 9.10. An event in a scenario-based diagram expressed with a FSM-based notation.

be to define multiple FSMs, one for each type of aspect. For each aspect, the complexity rises dramatically—making FSMs unwieldy. In other words, as an object can be classified as more things, the complexity of FSM representation increases.

- *When object behavior is not single threaded.* Objects can change in many ways. Such changes can often occur in any order and be asynchronous and concurrent. Since each FSM can only model an object in one state at a time, multiple and dynamic changes are not easily expressed. In these situations, a different technique is required.
- *When many kinds of objects interact.* Many objects and object types require many FSMs. A wall full of interconnected FSMs cannot be

easily comprehended. Under these circumstances, a different technique should be chosen.

- *When user experts find that FSMs do not describe their system in a useful manner.* Different problems require different techniques for solving them. No one technique can adequately express all system behavior. In addition to FSMs, rules and activity diagrams are other techniques that can be used to describe system behavior.

SUMMARY

Finite-state machines are a popular form for representing OO behavior, because FSMs can be readily mapped to OO programming languages. In an OO programming language, each FSM can be implemented with a class. Each FSM operation is then naturally associated with the class that implements the FSM.

FSM representations differ principally in where operations are expressed. When the operation is associated with the transition, the representation is known as the *Mealy model* of FSMs. When the operation is associated with the state, it is known as the *Moore model* of FSMs. Operations associated with both the state *and* the transition are called the *Mealy/Moore combination model*—a more flexible and robust model.

FSM-based diagrams provide one way of representing behavior. The behavior of several FSMs can be diagrammed on one piece of paper. However, *many* FSM diagrams on the same page would be overwhelming. Therefore, a different representation technique is required. One commonly used technique is the *object-type interaction* diagram. However, the scenario-based specification is also commonly used, because it expresses in the form of a script the state changes that involve *many* object types. In other words, object states and their state changes are still expressed—just in a different graphic form. Furthermore, the analyst does not have to choose just one specification technique. Since FSM- and scenario-based representations are state related, the segue from one kind of representation to another is relatively straightforward.

REFERENCES

Booch, Grady, *Object-Oriented Design with Applications,* Benjamin/Cummings, Redwood City, CA, 1991.

Booch, Grady, *Object-Oriented Analysis and Design with Applications* (2nd edition), Benjamin/Cummings, Redwood City, CA, 1994.

Coad, Peter and Edward Yourdon, *Object-Oriented Analysis* (2nd edition), Prentice-Hall, Englewood Cliffs, NJ, 1991.

Embley, David W., Barry N. Kurtz, and Scott N. Woodfield, *Object-Oriented Systems Analysis: A Model-Driven Approach,* Prentice-Hall, Englewood Cliffs, NJ, 1992.

Rumbaugh, James et al., *Object-Oriented Modeling and Design,* Prentice-Hall, Englewood Cliffs, NJ, 1991.

Shlaer, Sally and Stephen J. Mellor, *Object Life Cycles,* Prentice-Hall, Englewood Cliffs, NJ, 1991.

Part III
Business Rules

Business policies and conditions can be expressed using several different techniques. Often such expressions can be graphical, such as class diagrams, state-transition diagrams, and activity diagrams. Frequently, however, such diagrams are not expressive enough to represent all requirements of a system. For example, how can one of these diagrams express the following fact:

A Customer is a Bad Payer
IF AND ONLY IF the number of Invoices
(sent to this Customer and with Due Date before today)
is greater than 3.

Business rules can be used in many ways. The important points are

- they must express the business policies and conditions effectively,
- end users should be able to understand and express them,
- they need to be rigorous and formal so that they form a basis for code generation,
- they can be applied under all circumstances and at all times.

The articles in this section discuss what rules are as well as present ways in which rules can be used to supplement other techniques.

Business Rules

January 1995

The requirements of an enterprise can be specified using various techniques: object-relationship diagrams, class hierarchies, state-transition charts, event schemas, predicate logic, functional statements, production rules, and so on. The OO analyst/designer should choose the specification technique that best describes the problem at hand. When specifying the various states of a telephone call, a state-transition diagram is appropriate. A medical-diagnosis system can be specified using the production rules of an expert system. A stock analyst might use neural-network topology diagrams for a knotty bond-analysis problem. Another rapidly emerging technique is *rule* specification (sometimes called *business rules*). This column focuses on answering the following:

- What are rules and why do we need them?
- How can they be expressible in the end-user's natural language— while being, at the same time, both rigorous and formally defined?
- What is a useful way of categorizing rules?
- How can rules specify object structure as well as object behavior?
- Can certain rules be applied under some circumstances and not others?

INTRODUCTION TO RULES

Rules allow user experts to specify policies or conditions in small, stand-alone units using explicit statements.

> Rules are declarations of policy or conditions that must be satisfied. [OMG, 1992]

Organizational policies and conditions can be expressed in such declarations as the following:

> Pay a supplier invoice only if it has been approved.
> The product ordered from a supplier must be offered by this supplier.
> Put the orders of bad payers on a waiting list, until they pay the amounts due.
> A bad payer is a customer having more than three invoices overdue.

Rules, however, are not automatically justified, just because they provide an economical form of specification. If another technique is clearer, clarity of specification should be chosen over economy. (Coding is an entirely different story.) Therefore, if a user finds that a rule expresses a particular policy or condition more clearly, a rule should be used. The user, though, does not always have to choose between one technique or another. Rules can also be used to supplement other techniques, such as entity diagrams, dataflow diagrams, and state-transition diagrams.

RULES EXPRESSED IN NATURAL LANGUAGE

Rules need to be rigorous so that they form a basis for code generation. A typical rule expression in the language Prolog is:

> sister (x,y) : - female (x), parent (x,z), parent (y,z)

This statement means that x is the sister of y if x is female and x and y have the same parent z. Rules presented in this manner, however, will not be understood easily by most end users. Therefore, rules should also be expressible in the end-user's natural language—while being, at the same time, both rigorous and formally defined. Using this approach, the four rules above could be specified as follows:

> Pay Supplier Invoice
> ONLY IF its status is "Approved".
>
> IT MUST ALWAYS HOLD THAT
> a Product that is ordered from a Supplier
> is offered by this Supplier.
>
> WHEN requested to fill a Customer Order
> IF the Customer issuing this Customer Order is a Bad Payer
> THEN put this Customer Order on a Waiting List.

WHEN a Customer ceases to be a Bad Payer
THEN process backorders for this Customer.

A Customer is a Bad Payer
IF AND ONLY IF the number of Invoices
(sent to this Customer and with Due Date before today)
is greater than 3.

When defined in this way, rules go beyond being just explicit statements of policy. Rules can also be executable specifications for an automated system. Therefore, when a business changes its rules, its automation operates differently. Such rules do not just reflect the business, they *are* the business. Rules, then, should be

- executable declarations of policies or conditions.
- understandable by the user community.

Until recently, this was science fiction. However, the automated support for executable and user-understandable rules is now available.

CATEGORIES OF RULES

Rules can be classified in many ways. One technique divides rules initially into two categories: constraint rules and derivation rules. Constraint rules specify policies or conditions that restrict object structure and behavior. Derivation rules specify policies or conditions for inferring or computing facts from other facts [Gray, 1992]. Beyond these two types of rules, further categorization can be defined:

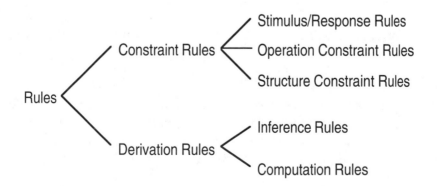

Again, rules can be classified in many ways. The categorization, above, was chosen because it reflects one way in which users think about rule specification. There is nothing holy about it. This categorization is just one useful approach to organize the presentation of rules in this book.

Stimulus/Response Rules

Stimulus/response rules constrain behavior by specifying WHEN and IF conditions that must be true in order for an operation to be triggered. Examples of stimulus/response rule are:

> WHEN the stock level of a Product becomes less than the reorder point
> THEN reorder this Product.

> WHEN a Library Book is requested by a Borrower
> IF Copy of Library Book is available
> THEN check out this Copy to this Borrower
> ELSE place next available Copy of this Library Book on reserve.

Stimulus/response rules constrain behavior within an event context. In other words, the rule's IF condition only holds WHEN a particular type of event occurs. Therefore, the IF condition for an operation can differ by event stimulus. For instance, a Close Order operation can be invoked under the following conditions:

> WHEN Order shipped or Order paid events occur
> IF Order is paid and Order is shipped
> THEN Close Order.

> WHEN an Order cancelled event occurred
> IF Order is cancelled and Order is not shipped
> THEN Close Order.

When an IF condition must be true for an operation to perform correctly (no matter what type of event occurs), a different kind of rule is required.

Operation Constraint Rules

Operation constraint rules specify those conditions that must hold before and after an operation to ensure that the operation performs correctly. Such constraints are vital to the execution of an operation and are completely independent of the event context under which the operation is invoked. Bertrand Meyer states that the presence of these rules should be viewed as a contract that binds a method and its requestors. Here, the operation says "if you call me with the precondition satisfied, I promise to deliver a final state in which the postcondition is satisfied" [Meyer, 1988].

Operation precondition rules express those constraints under which an operation will perform correctly. The operation cannot go ahead unless these constraints are met. Examples of this kind of rule are:

Promote Staff employee to Manager
    ONLY IF this Employee is not a Manager.

Marry a Male and a Female
    ONLY IF this Female is not married
      and this Male is not married.

In contrast, *operation postcondition rules* guarantee the results. This kind of rule says that when an operation is executed, a certain state must result. Examples of this kind of rule are:

Promote Staff employee to Manager IS CORRECTLY COMPLETED
    ONLY IF this Employee is a Manager.

Marry a Male and a Female IS CORRECTLY COMPLETED
    ONLY IF this Female is married
    and this Male is married
    and this Female is married to this Male.

Structure Constraint Rules

Structure constraint rules specify policies or conditions about object types and their associations that should not be violated. A rule can constrain object structure in many ways.

A rule can constrain the value of an attribute:

IT MUST ALWAYS HOLD THAT
    an Employee's salary cannot be greater than her manager's salary.

A rule can constrain the population of an object type:

IT MUST ALWAYS HOLD THAT
    the number of U.S. Supreme Court Justices must not be greater than 9.

A rule can constrain the cardinality of a relationship:

IT MUST ALWAYS HOLD THAT
  a Probationary Customer may place no more than 7 Orders.

Other examples of structure constraint rules are as follows:

IT MUST ALWAYS HOLD THAT
  the number of Employees
  (who are Managers and earning a Salary greater than 100,000)
  is less than or equal to 3.

IT MUST ALWAYS HOLD THAT
  for any given Life Insurance Policy
  the Policyholder is not the same as the Beneficiary.

IT MUST ALWAYS HOLD THAT
  every Person is a Male Person or a Female Person.

IT MUST ALWAYS HOLD THAT
  every Flight that is scheduled to depart from a City
  is not scheduled to arrive in this City.

IT MUST ALWAYS HOLD THAT
  The sum of salaries of employees working for a Department
  is less than 0.6 * budget of this Department.

Structure constraint rules omit references to operations, because they must hold under any operational circumstance. In other words, whenever an object's state is changed (whether this change is creation, termination, or modification), its structure constraint rules must hold. For instance, whenever an employee is added or an employee's age changes, the following rule is enforced:

IT MUST ALWAYS HOLD THAT
  an Employee's age cannot be greater than 75.

Inference Rules

Inference rules specify that if certain facts are true, a conclusion can be inferred. As such, they generally have an IF . . . THEN form. Such rules are generally associated with expert systems. Examples of inference rules are:

IF an object is an Employee
THEN that object is an Person.

IF a Polygon has a perimeter
THEN a Square has a perimeter.

Rules with inferences in both directions can also be specified in an IF AND ONLY IF form.

An inference rule can derive object subtypes:

A Person is an Employee IF AND ONLY IF
    this Person works for an Organization.

A Customer is a Bad Payer IF AND ONLY IF
    the number of Invoices
        (sent to this Customer and with a due date before today)
    is greater than 3.

An inference rule can derive object associations:

An Employee reports to a Manager IF AND ONLY IF
    this Employee works for Department
    that is headed by this Manager.

Computation Rules

Inference rules execute derivation merely by accessing available facts. In contrast, computation rules derive their results via processing algorithms. Computation rules can be thought of as inferences. The primary difference, however, is the manner of expressing the derivation. The inference rule is a rule conceived in an IF. . . THEN manner. The computation rule is a rule conceived as an equation. Some examples of computation rules are as follows:

A rule can specify value computation:

The net price of a Product IS COMPUTED AS FOLLOWS
    product price * (1 + tax percentage / 100).

A rule can specify the computation of object types:

The object type Woman IS COMPUTED AS FOLLOWS
    the intersection of all Female Humans and Adult Humans.

A rule can specify the computation of associations:

The parent association IS COMPUTED AS FOLLOWS
    the union of both the mother and father associations.

Computation rules can appear to be just another structure constraint rule, because both have an IT MUST ALWAYS HOLD quality. Structure constraints, however, are rules expressed in terms of conditional statements that must be true. Computation rules are expressed in terms of how something is derived from something else. For the OO programmer, both just become methods in a class. To a user, they describe different ways of thinking about and specifying business rules.

GLOBAL, LOCAL, AND TEMPORAL APPLICATION OF RULES

The rules presented above may or may not be applied under all circumstances and at all times. For instance, the following rules would usually be in effect:

A Person is an Employee IF AND ONLY IF
  this Person works for an Organization.

Promote Staff employee to Manager IS CORRECTLY COMPLETED
  ONLY IF this Employee is a Manager.

However, some rules may have certain restrictions on the processing scope to which they apply.

(global unless otherwise overridden locally)
IT MUST ALWAYS HOLD THAT
  an Order must have 1 or more Line Items.
(during order acceptance)
IT MUST ALWAYS HOLD THAT
  an Order can have 0 or more Line Items.

Rule applicability may also depend on cultural and legal policies in force at various locations.

(In Omaha, Nebraska)
Marry a Male and a Female
  ONLY IF this Female is not married
    and this Male is not married.
(In Tibet)
Marry a Male and a Female
  ONLY IF this Male is not married.

Whether a rule is applicable may also depend upon the element of time.

(Before 1/1/92)
WHEN an Order is shipped and the Order is paid
THEN close Order.

(As of 1/1/92)
WHEN an Order is shipped and the Order is paid and 60 days have elapsed
THEN close Order.

SUMMARY

Business policies and conditions can be expressed using several different techniques. Often such expressions can be graphical, though sometimes an explicit declarative statement is a better vehicle. Combining both techniques is also advantageous and will be presented in another article. This column has explored five categories of rules that can specify business policies and conditions using such statements. The categories presented here are just one way to think about rule taxonomy. Rules can be categorized in many other ways. The important points are

- rules must express the business policies and conditions effectively.
- end users should be able to understand and express them.
- rules need to be rigorous and formal so that they form a basis for code generation.
- rules can be applied under all circumstances and at all times.

REFERENCES

Gray, Peter M. D., Krishnarao G. Kulkarni, and Norman W. Paton, *Object-Oriented Databases: A Semantic Data Model Approach,* Prentice-Hall, New York, 1992.

Meyer, Bertrand, *Object-Oriented Software Construction,* Prentice-Hall, New York, 1988.

Object Management Group (OMG), *Object-Oriented Analysis and Design, Reference Model,* Draft 7.0, unofficial position from OOA&D SIG, 1992.

Using Rules
with Diagrams

February 1995

R ules allow user experts to specify policies or conditions in small, stand-
alone units using explicit statements. This article presents ways in
which rules can be used to supplement other techniques, such as object-relationship diagrams, process-dependency diagrams, and event diagrams.
This article focuses on answering the following questions:

- Can diagrams be used instead of language-like rules?
- When should rules be used instead of or in addition to diagrams?
- How can rules be used in an object-oriented manner?
- Can rules be executable and readable at the same time?

USING RULES AND/OR DIAGRAMS

Policies and conditions can be represented in various ways. For example,
Fig. 11.1(a) expresses the business policy that an Order can be placed by one
and only one Customer. In other words, this business constraint is stated
solely using symbols on the relationship line of an object-relationship diagram. The same constraint can also be expressed as a declarative statement or *rule* (Fig. 11.1(b)). Either expression can be used to represent the
business policy—that an Order is placed by one and only one Customer. Both
examples express this business policy with the same degree of accuracy.
Passed to a code generator, either representation should produce the same
results. Which form of representation should be used by the OO analyst?
As long as each form produces the same results, the choice should be based
on clarity of representation.

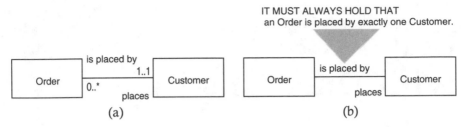

Figure 11.1.   Two ways of expressing a business policy on order placement.

While the business policy in Fig. 11.1 could easily be expressed as an English-based* language rule or as symbols on a line, both options are not always appropriate. Often, a policy or condition is too cumbersome to express (and read) as graphic symbols. In such situations, English-based language rules should be explored as a possible alternative representation. For example, Fig. 11.2 depicts several business policies and conditions. (*Where* to attach rule statements graphically will be discussed later.) Those that involve more complex representations, such as computations and condition checking, are expressed as rules. However, not every constraint in Fig. 11.2 is expressed as a rule. For example, the constraint that an employee must work for exactly one department is expressed with a "1...1" on the left of the relationship line. In other words, policies and conditions can be represented using rules *and* graphic symbols. The analyst is then free to choose a mixture of representations.

Figure 11.3 depicts two ways of expressing the same business policy—that once an order is assembled, its shipment process should begin. As with Fig. 11.1, either representation can be used to communicate this business policy. Figure 11.3(b) illustrates an event diagram depicting two operations Assemble Order and Ship Order. When an Assemble Order operation is completed, an Order assembled event occurs—triggering a Ship Order operation. Figure 11.3(a) is an English-based rule statement expressing the stimulus/response dynamics of Fig. 11.3(b). In the case of simple stimulus/response policies, such as those in Fig. 11.3, perhaps the English-based rule form is clearer and easier to use. However, in more complex stimulus/response chains (as depicted in Fig. 11.4), a graphic form might be more appropriate.

---

* While *English-based language* is not multiculturally correct, the term *natural language* carries with it all sorts of AI baggage. A term such as *form-of language-similar-to-the-way-humans-speak* would be more accurate, but cumbersome.

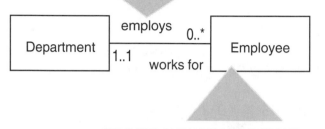

IT MUST ALWAYS HOLD THAT
  the number of Employees that a Department employs
      (who are managers and
      have a salary greater than 100,000)
  is less than or equal to 3.

IT MUST ALWAYS HOLD THAT
    the sum of salaries of all Employees
    that works for a Department
    is less than 0.6 ∗ Budget of this Department.

Figure 11.2. Constraints expressed as numeric symbols and English-based rules.

RULES AND OO

Rules are not always used in conjunction with diagrams. For example, a user could just state the following rule without any accompanying diagram:

> Promote to Manager
> ONLY IF this Employee is not a Manager.

However, if rules are not classified in some manner, huge vats of unorganized "rule soup" can result—making reusability difficult. One solution to rule organization is indexing each (either directly or indirectly) around a type of object. For example, the declaration of the rule above can be associated with the Promote to Manager operation. In turn, the Promote to Manager is probably an operation on Employee objects. By implication, this rule is an Employee-related feature. (In an OO implementation, the rule would be part of the encapsulation of Order class objects.) Therefore, the OO analyst must somehow make such associations explicit. Most repositories have their own language-based syntax. However, associations can also be graphic, such as that depicted in Fig. 11.5. Alternatively, the analyst could use paper and pencil to indicate off-page connectors or use an OO-CASE tool via

WHEN Order assembled
  THEN Ship Order.

Assemble Order — Order assembled → Ship Order

(a)   (b)

Figure 11.3.   Two ways of expressing the same stimulus/response policy.

mouse clicks and GUIs. While graphic associations are not necessary, they often improve communication and understanding. In the following section, several examples are given in which rules can be attached to diagrams.

ATTACHING RULES TO DIAGRAMS

Operation Constraint Rules

Wherever possible, rules should be attached to existing diagrams in a graphically appropriate place. For instance, operation constraint rules can be attached to diagrams depicting operations. The diagram in Fig. 11.6 depicts the Marry Couple operation annotated with pre- and postcondition operation constraints. (These diagrams could be a process dependency, a dataflow, or an event diagram.) No matter which context or circumstance surrounds the Marry Couple operation, the operation constraints must *always* apply.

Stimulus/Response Rules

The operation constraint rule is an integral part of an operation's functionality. Every time an operation is invoked, its operation constraint applies. In contrast, the stimulus/response rule is external to the opera-

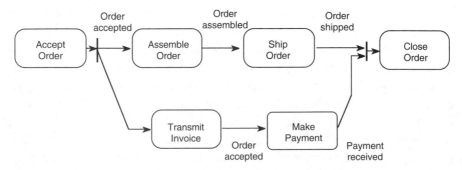

Figure 11.4.   In more complex chains of stimulus/response policies, graphic symbols communicate more effectively.

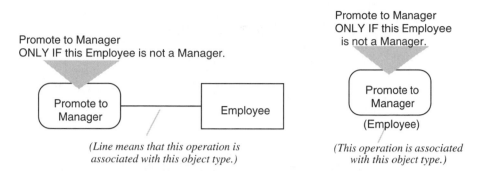

Figure 11.5. Stand-alone rules should be associated with object types in some manner.

tion. The operation does not need to know what *causes* the operation or what occurs *after* the operation. By treating the operation as a component, it can be plugged into one processing scenario after another—without requiring a change to the operation's method.

The event diagram in Fig. 11.7(a) is annotated with a stimulus/response rule. This rule is attached to the vertical bar control-condition symbol. Control conditions govern whether or not an operation should be invoked when triggered. In other words, the Close Sale operation can be potentially invoked when either a Product dispensed or Change dispensed event occurs. The control condition ensures that the Close Sale operation does not proceed unless a product is dispensed and the correct change is given. In Fig. 11.7(a), the WHEN and THEN (the *stimulus* and *response*) portions are documented both in the rule statement and diagram. The IF (or *control condition*) portion is only documented within the rule statement. Graphically attaching the rule to the vertical bar was done solely for clarity. When a stimulus/response rule has no IF portion, the rule can be graphically attached to a trigger line as depicted in Fig. 11.7(b).

Again, the stimulus/response rule is part of a processing scenario statement and not part of the Close Sale operation. In another processing scenario, a repair person may hit an "Emergency Override" button—*immediately* closing whatever sale may be in progress. In this scenario, correct change may not be given and a product may not be dispensed, yet the Close Sale operation is still invoked (that is, no IF condition is required).

Computation Rules

Computation rules can be attached to those portions of a diagram that are to be derived. For instance in Fig. 11.8, the slash mark on the relationship

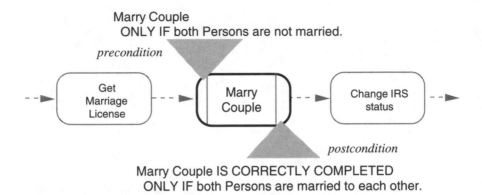

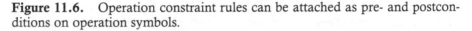

Marry Couple IS CORRECTLY COMPLETED
ONLY IF both Persons are married to each other.

Figure 11.6. Operation constraint rules can be attached as pre- and postconditions on operation symbols.

line labeled Person.has biological parents symbolizes that the association can be derived. (The box below Person indicates each Person object is subtyped as either a Male Person or a Female Person—and not both.) The actual computation of the has biological parents association is based on determining the mother and father of a given person separately using the has biological mother and has biological father associations. The results, taken together, are the person's biological parents. In Fig. 11.8, this computation is expressed as an English-based language rule attached to the appropriate relationship line.

Computation rules can also be attached to object types in an object diagram. The diagram in Fig. 11.9 indicates a Person is employed by any number of Organizations. In addition, it indicates that each Person is subtyped as either an Employee or a Nonemployee. The slash mark on the Employee object type symbolizes that the set of Employee objects can be computed. As the attached rule indicates, Employee objects are those Person objects associated to an Organization via the employed by association.

Structure Constraint Rules

As seen in Figs. 11.1 and 11.2 above, structure constraint rules can be attached to relationship lines or to object-type rectangles. Choosing which symbol to attach to a given rule is sometimes unclear. For instance in Fig. 11.1(b), the constraint clearly belongs on the relationship line because the rule is an association constraint. In Fig. 11.10, however, the choice is not so obvious. Are Flight objects being constrained or are the associations between Flight and City being constrained? Attaching the rule to Flight certainly makes sense, because departure and arrival information can be seen as

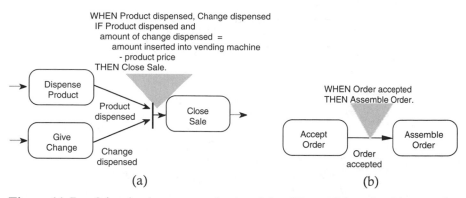

Figure 11.7. Stimulus/response rules involving IF condition checking can be graphically attached to control condition symbols. Without IF conditions, they can be attached to triggers.

properties of Flight objects. The constraint specification, therefore, should somehow become part of a method associated with the Flight object type.

On the other hand, attaching the rule to the relationship lines certainly makes visual sense, because it is the association between flights and cities that is being constrained. However, should the rule be attached to one or both of the lines? Keep in mind that attaching the rule to only one line does not omit the other relationship from being constrained as well. Since the rule cites both associations, *both* are implicated. Attaching the rule to

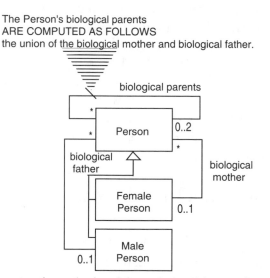

Figure 11.8. Computation rules involving relationships can be attached to relationship lines.

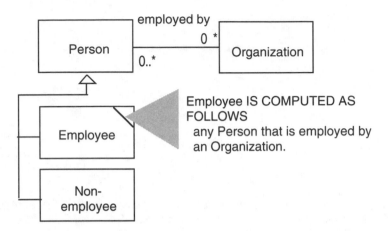

Figure 11.9.   Computation rules involving object types can be attached to object-type rectangles.

a line is only a graphic communication device. At design and construction time, the association constraint involves two mappings from Flight objects to City objects. Therefore, the code that embodies this constraint must address both associations. This helps the OO designer ensure that the rule-support code becomes part of those methods within the Flight class that maintain arrival and departure associations. (Moreover, to maintain structural integrity, an inverse method should also be generated for the City class.) In short, regardless of the graphic symbol to which this rule is attached, the same result should occur.

Structure constraint rules can also be used in those diagramming approaches that incorporate the notion of attribute type. For example, Fig. 11.11 depicts an Employee object type with attributes title, salary, and so on. Here, the salary attribute type is constrained via the attached rule. At OO development time, this guides the designer to define an instance-variable method that adequately enforces the indicated salary business rule.

RULE SYNTAX: EXECUTABILITY VERSUS READABILITY

Rules often end up with a syntax that is less than optimal for human understanding. For instance in Fig. 11.12, the rule on the top states that the is held by Person is not the same as the is paid to Person. Treating verb phrases such as "is held by" as adjectives is not typical English usage. Rules such as these can

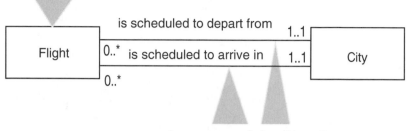

IT MUST ALWAYS HOLD THAT
every Flight that is scheduled to depart from a City
is not scheduled to arrive in this City.

(or use same rule here instead)

Figure 11.10. Constraint rules involving relationships can be attached to the relationship lines and/or the object-type boxes, yet yield the same result.

easily be misunderstood by end users. Therefore, to increase clarity, rules should also be expressible in the end-user's language—while remaining both rigorous and formally defined. One solution, used by IntelliCorp's OMW OO-CASE tool, is syntax substitution. For instance, an end user might decide that the words "is held by Person" would be understood better as "policyholder" and the "is paid to Person" as "beneficiary." In this

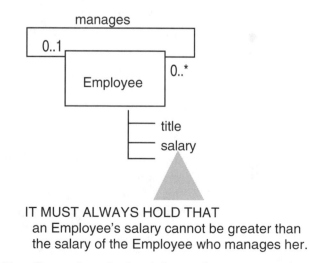

IT MUST ALWAYS HOLD THAT
an Employee's salary cannot be greater than
the salary of the Employee who manages her.

Figure 11.11. Constraint rules involving attribute types can be attached to the attribute name.

for executability:

IT MUST ALWAYS HOLD THAT
for any given Life Insurance Policy
the is held by Person is not the same as
the is paid to Person.

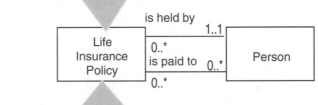

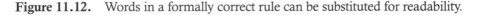

or, for readability:

IT MUST ALWAYS HOLD THAT
for any given Life Insurance Policy
the *policyholder* is not the same as
the *beneficiary*.

Figure 11.12.   Words in a formally correct rule can be substituted for readability.

way, a more readable version would be the rule on the bottom of Fig. 11.12 stating that the *policyholder* is not the same as the *beneficiary*.

Here, syntax substitution does not mean *discarding* one syntax for another. Rather, for *user presentation* one syntax is used instead of another. The original syntax remains, because tools such as OMW require the formalism to automate the rule. The presentation syntax remains so that it can be readily understood by nontechnically inclined people. In other words, both versions are maintained so that both executability and readability are supported.

SUMMARY

Rules allow user experts to specify policies or conditions in small, stand-alone units using explicit statements. This article presents ways in which rules can be used to supplement other techniques, such as object-relationship diagrams, process-dependency diagrams, and event diagrams.

The physical portrayal used in this article to attach rules to diagrams is not important. What is important is that business policies and conditions can be represented using rules *and* graphic symbols. The analyst is then free to choose a mixture of representation techniques. As long as the resulting execution is the same, this choice should be based on the mixture of techniques that yields the greatest clarity.

Part IV
Object Complexity

When we look out at the world, we see many objects. As humans, we try to make sense of this highly populated world by organizing our objects in various ways. Thus, we do not have to deal with each object individually, but by *groups* of objects. This section introduces three notions that we use to group objects: classification, generalization, and aggregation. While there are others, such as the prototype and coalesce mechanisms, these three are the most common on OO analysis. (Since aggregation is fairly new to the modeling scene, additional material on it is presented in the next section.)

The material in this section appears as two articles, because one article was too long for a single issue.

Managing Object Complexity Part I: Classification and Generalization

September 1992

We live in a complex world. Even the simple tasks of life would be confusing without the proper mental tools. One of these tools is the acquisition of concepts. Concepts result from our ability to *classify*. Once we form these classifications, we can further organize our world by distinguishing when one classification is more general than another. This allows us to build hierarchies of *generalizations*. Additionally, we can *compose* a single object from a configuration of other objects. These kinds of mechanisms are part of our human endowment and enable us to grasp and manage the complexity of our world. In object-oriented analysis, we can use them to model our enterprise world.

While we employ many mechanisms for managing object complexity, this article explains and demystifies two of these mechanisms: classification and generalization. There is nothing magic or mighty about them. At their heart, classification and generalization are just relations that involve concepts and their objects. Furthermore, we can model these relations as we would any other relation.

CLASSIFICATION

Each object is unique. However, classification removes certain distinctions, so that we can see commonalities between objects. Without classification, we would only know that each thing is different. With classification, we selectively omit certain distinguishing features of one or more objects, thus allowing us to concentrate on the features they do share.

> *Classification* is the act or result of removing certain distinctions between objects, so that we can see commonalities.

In Fig. 12.1, the little person is classifying various objects in his realm. Even though each object is different, the objects on the top share the properties of being milk containers made of a heavy waxed paper. This classification is named "milk carton."

Objects do not form sets by themselves. The process of classification does this. Two things having the same abstracted form are analogous. These abstracted forms can be called concepts or—in more standard terminology—*object types.* This means that the little man's classification of waxy carton objects is another way of saying that he has determined that there is a type of object called Milk Carton. In short, all objects to which the same object type applies are analogous. [Langer, 1967]

In Fig. 12.2, the dashed and arrowed lines indicate the direction of classification. Here, the objects named Jane and Jasper are abstracted. They are classified as Person objects. In another classification process, the objects named Jane and IBM are classified as Property Owner objects. Person and Property Owner, then, are two concepts that result from classification processes.

Figure 12.1. Classification removes certain distinctions among objects and result in concepts.

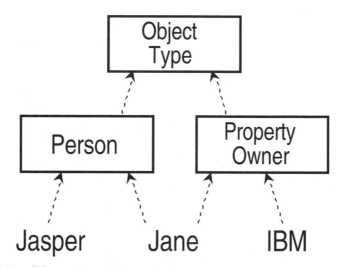

Figure 12.2.   Hierarchies of classification can be defined.

However, Person and Property Owner are also objects: they are classified as Object Type objects.

Classification is one way we manage the complexity of the objects in the world. It allows us to treat many individual phenomena with a single notion. Therefore, the result of classification is an object type. In other words—as indicated in Fig. 12.3—classification is a relation between object types and objects. It specifies that each Object Type can be instantiated by 0, 1, or many Objects. (Yes, a concept may or may not have instances.) In addition, it specifies that each Object must be classified as 1 or more Object Types. (According to many psychologists and philosophers, an object without a classification cannot be perceived. According to OO programming, an object without a class cannot be created or manipulated.)

GENERALIZATION

When we look in our clothes closet, we recognize the objects we see as slacks, shirts, coats, shoes, rollerblades, bolo ties, etc. Without well-developed generalizing capabilities, we might call this storage area, the shoes-slacks-shirts-coats-rollerblades . . . closet. The more kinds of things we have in the closet, the more cumbersome the name becomes. Generalization enables us to examine whether these concepts have anything in common. Is there a *more general* concept that encompasses concepts such as Shoe,

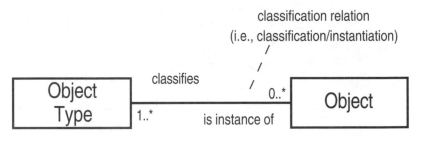

Figure 12.3.   Classification is a relation between concepts and objects.

Slacks, and Shirt? In *general,* these are known as Clothing. Clothing, in turn, might be incorporated into an even more general category called Merchandise or Household Article—and so on. In other words, generalization itself is not a classification: it distinguishes *between* classifications.

> *Generalization* is the act or result of distinguishing one type of object that is more encompassing than another.*

Generalization enables us to say that all instances of a specific object type are also instances of a more general object type—but, not necessarily the other way around. For example, all Shoe or Shirt objects are also Clothing objects, but not all Clothing objects are Shoe or Shirt objects. Therefore, Clothing is a more general concept than Shoe or Shirt. Whatever makes Shoes different from Shirts is not addressed in the definition of Clothing. Only their commonality is recognized.

With generalization, we can define hierarchies of object types, forming more and more general object types. Figure 12.4 shows that a Lifeform is a more general kind of object (or *supertype*) than a Human, that Human is more general than Female Human, that, in turn, is more general than Girl.

The opposite of generalization is *specialization.* For example, Human can be *specialized* as Female Human or Male Human; or as Infant, Adolescent, or Adult Human; and Good, Bad, or Ugly Human. These specialized concepts are *subtypes.* In Fig. 12.4, Girl is a subtype of Female Human, Female Human is a subtype of Human, and so on.

---

* The term generalization has other meanings, and this act or result has other names. The pairing of this word and definition, however, is typical.

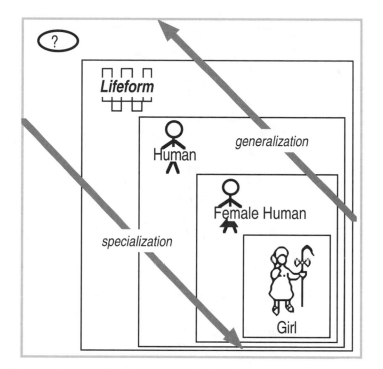

Figure 12.4.   A generalization/specialization hierarchy.

One way of thinking about generalization is picturing sets of objects within sets of objects. Figure 12.5 depicts Jane as an instance of the object types Woman and Employee. Woman and Employee, in turn, are both specializations of the more general Person object type. This means that the concept of Person applies to Jane as well.

Confusion between classification and generalization is common. For example, we say that Jane is a Woman as well as Woman is a Person. The former is classification and the latter generalization. Yet, we use the words "is a" for both. This is a problem that dates back (at least) to Plato and Aristotle. Only in the nineteenth century did the mathematician Peano finally clarify this issue. Essentially, he declared that classification and generalization are two different relations. Classification defines an "is instance of" relation (Fig. 12.3); generalization defines an "is subtype of" relation (Fig. 12.5). (Mathematicians use the symbols ∈ and ⊂, respectively.) In other words, "is a" should not be used; instead, "is instance of" or "is kind of" should be used. Figure 12.8 illustrates how both relations can be used at the same time.

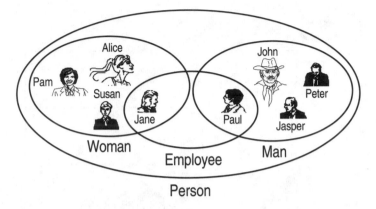

Figure 12.5. Generalization as sets that encompass other sets.

> *Generalization* is the act or result of removing certain types of distinctions between types of objects, so that we can see commonalities.

Generalization enables us to define our concepts in even more general terms by using supertypes. The inverse, specialization, allows us to be more specific about our concepts by using subtypes. The notation in Fig. 12.7 is one way of specifying the generalization (and specialization) relation. As Fig. 12.3 can be thought of as a meta-model specification for the diagram in Fig. 12.2, Fig. 12.7 can be thought of as a meta-model specification for the diagram in Fig. 12.6.

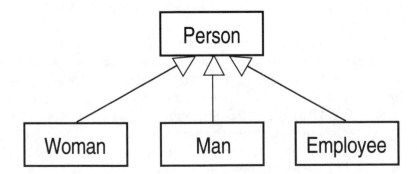

Figure 12.6. Directions of generalization between concepts.

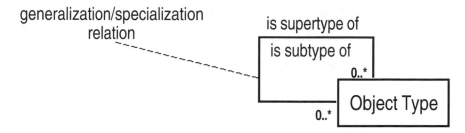

Figure 12.7. Generalization/specialization is a relation defining subtypes and supertypes.

SUMMARY

This article focuses on two of the mechanisms analysts can employ to cope with the complexity inherent in our world of objects.

Classification removes certain distinctions, so that we can see commonalities between objects. Without classification, we would only know that everything is different. With classification, we manage complexity using the concepts we form which result from classification.

The second mechanism is *generalization.* Generalization distinguishes a concept that is more general than another. It enables us to say that all

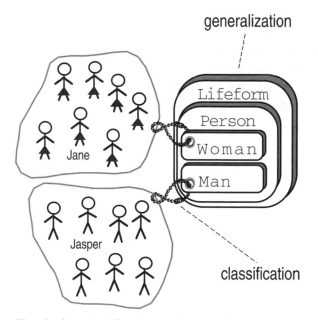

Figure 12.8. Employing classification and generalization at the same time.

instances of a more specific concept are also instances of a general concept—but not necessarily the other way around. With generalization, we can build hierarchies (lattices) of concepts, forming more and more general concepts. The opposite of generalization is *specialization*. As Fig. 12.8 indicates, we can and do employ these mechanisms separately or together.

REFERENCES

Abiteboul, Serge and Richard Hull, "IFO: A Formal Semantic Database Model," *ACM Transactions on Database Systems,* 12:4, December 1987, pp. 525–565.

Bolton, Neil, *Concept Formation,* Pergamon Press, Oxford, 1977.

Borgida, Alexander T. et al., "Generalization/Specialization as a Basis for Software Specification," *On Conceptual Modelling,* Michael L. Brodie et al. eds., Springer-Verlag, New York, 1984, pp. 87–117.

Brodie, M. L. and D. Ridjanovic, "On the Design and Specification of Database Transactions," *On Conceptual Modelling: Perspectives from Artificial Intelligence, Databases, and Programming Languages,* Michael L. Brodie et al. eds., Springer-Verlag, New York, 1984, pp. 277–312.

Daintith, John and R. D. Nelson ed., *Dictionary of Mathematics,* Penguin Books, London, 1989.

Flew, Anthony, *A Dictionary of Philosophy,* (2nd revised edition), Macmillan Press, London, 1984.

Langer, Susanne K., *An Introduction to Symbolic Logic,* (3rd edition), Dover Publications, New York, 1967.

Smith, John M. and Diane C. P. Smith, "Database Classifications: Aggregation and Generalization," *ACM Transactions on Database Systems,* 2:2, June 1977, pp. 105–13.

Sowa, J. F., *Conceptual Structures,* Addison-Wesley, Reading, Mass, 1984.

Managing Object Complexity Part II: Aggregation

September 1992

A s suggested in the previous article, we live in a complex world. Even the simple tasks of life would be confusing without the proper mental tools. As humans, we employ several kinds of mechanisms to grasp and manage the complexity of our world. Our ability to *classify* results in object types. Once we form these classifications, we can further organize our world by distinguishing when one classification is more encompassing than another. This allows us to build hierarchies of *generalizations.* Additionally, we can *aggregate* a single object from a configuration of other objects.

The previous article explored the mechanisms of classification and generalization. In particular, it discussed that their meta-model definitions specify relations involving the notions of Object Type and Object. Classification is expressed as a relation that links an Object Type to its Object instances. Generalization is expressed as a relation that defines a subtype/supertype association between two Object Types. In this article, the mechanism of aggregation and its meta-model foundation will be discussed.

AGGREGATION

Aggregation is a mechanism for forming a whole from component parts. For example, aggregation can configure assembled structures, such as each Sailboat consists of its Hull, Sail, and Engine (Fig. 13.1) or each Hammer consists of its Head and Handle. Other aggregations can be more conceptual and subjective in nature, such as each Trade Union is a collection of its Employee members or each Record is consists of its Field Values.

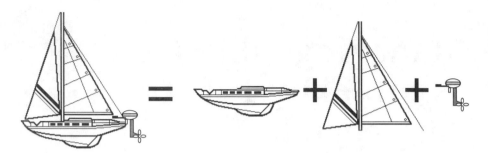

Figure 13.1. Aggregation can indicate configurations of assembly structures.

> *Aggregation* is the act or result of forming an object config-
> ured from its component parts; it is a part-whole relation.

Notice that the aggregations above, of Sailboat, Hammer, and so on, are
expressed in terms of object types. This does not mean that these object
types are composed of other "component" object types. It means that the
instances of these object types are composed of *instances* of other object
types (as illustrated in Fig. 13.2). While aggregation is based on objects
consisting of other objects, defining aggregation solely in terms of objects
is literally meaningless. To understand objects, we need the applicable
object types. In other words, if an object has no applicable object types, we
have no way of understanding how to perceive and manipulate it. Therefore, we need to specify the way in which *types* of objects consist of other
types of objects (Fig. 13.2).

Figure 13.3, then, is one way to model the composed object in Fig. 13.1.
This diagram expresses the underlying object types, or types of objects,
depicted in Fig. 13.1.

Additionally, component parts might in turn have their own component parts. Therefore, the Engine in the Sailboat could consist of various Pistons, Rods, Valves, and an Engine Block. In this way, aggregation can define hierarchies of part-whole configurations.

Some Thoughts on our Use of Aggregation

Aggregation reduces complexity by treating a configuration of many things
as one. For instance, we treat each Human Body object as one, even though
it is a configuration of other objects, such as Arms, Legs, a Head, a Heart,

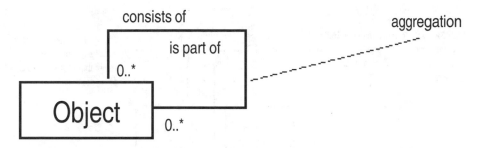

Figure 13.2.   Aggregation specifies that an object of one type can consist of—and can be part of—objects of other types.

and so on. When treated in this manner, many of the properties of the whole can apply to its parts as well. For example, if a Human Body is moved from one location to another, its component parts are also moved. If a Human Body is rotated, we can reasonably assume that the body's components are rotated as well. However, not all the properties of an object are seemingly "inherited" by—or propagated to—its components. For example, a delete operation on a Human Body could also be propagated to include all its parts. However, deleting a Trade Union would probably not include deleting its Employee members. Therefore, such implications should be defined for each aggregation. In fact, such propagation should be considered on a level-by-level basis. For example, if a Thumb is a part of a Person, and a Person is part of a Community, is the Thumb part of the Community? Furthermore, does an operation applied to a Community and propagated to a Person also apply to the Thumb?

We use aggregation when we wish to address a whole rather than its parts. In addition, our choice of when and how we employ aggregation is highly subjective. For example, a Human Body is constantly replacing its Cell components. Even though Jane is not composed of the same objects from one moment to the next, somehow we still consider the particular aggregation to be Jane. Similarly, if your Car lost a Windshield Wiper or one of its Tires were replaced, would it be the same Car object?

Aggregation brings up an assortment of questions about how we compose and recognize complex objects. We allow certain components of an object to change over time, yet define other components to remain immutable. For example, a particular married couple consists of a husband and wife. Neither of these components can be removed without destroying the couple. (Here, the delete operation is propagated from a

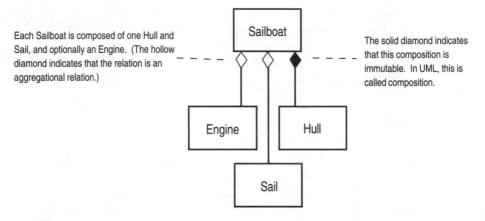

Each Sailboat is composed of one Hull and Sail, and optionally an Engine. (The hollow diamond indicates that the relation is an aggregational relation.)

The solid diamond indicates that this composition is immutable. In UML, this is called composition.

Figure 13.3.   The types of objects composed in Fig. 13.1 (i.e., the underlying object types).

part to its whole—instead of the other way around.) Each married couple, therefore, is an immutably composite object whose classification results in the object type Marriage. This notion is know as *composition.*

Figure 13.3 is an example of a hybrid aggregation where the sailboat's engine and sail are changeable, yet its hull is immutable. In this situation, if the hull is removed, the original sailboat can no longer exist. However, the sailboat's sail and engine can change without terminating the Sailboat object.

COMPOSITION

> *Composition* is the act or result of forming an object
> that is *immutably* configured from its component parts.

This invariant form of aggregation can define instances like those of marriages, airline reservations, or desk assignments. Each immutably composed object is created solely on the basis of its immutable component parts. Once created, an object cannot change these components. If it did, it would, by definition, become a different object.

The best way to understand composition is by looking at why anyone might want to create a complex object with immutable components. Figure 13.4 contains several Man and Woman objects. During the course of systems analysis, the analyst may wish to refer to certain pairs of people,

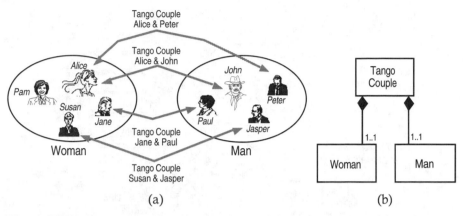

Figure 13.4.   Instances of tango couples and their components (a) and a way of expressing it in UML (b).

where each pair must contain one object from each gender. These pairs may be assembled for a tango competition, for a marriage ceremony, or whatever reality the analyst perceives. The important point is that the analyst wishes to refer to this man-woman object pair as a purposeful unit. For example, "Tango Couple Jane and Paul" refers to the dancing duo comprising "Jane" and "Paul." "Tango Couple Alice and John" is a singular collective reference to the dancers "Alice" and "John"; and so on. In this way, "Alice" and "John" (while free to be components in other aggregations) are considered the immutable components of the complex object "Tango Couple Alice and John." Immutable components can be thought of as "defining" a composition, because if another object were substituted, a *different* tango couple would be defined. If either object were removed, the pairing would cease to exist. Each of these couples, then, is immutably formed on the basis of two specific objects.

SUMMARY

As humans, we employ many other mechanisms that help us handle complexity. For instance, the *coalesce* mechanism helps us treat several objects as the *same* object. The *prototype* mechanism helps us define the similarity of one object with a prototype object. While we employ many mechanisms for managing object complexity, the purpose of this article is to explain and demystify three of these mechanisms: classification, generalization, and aggregation.

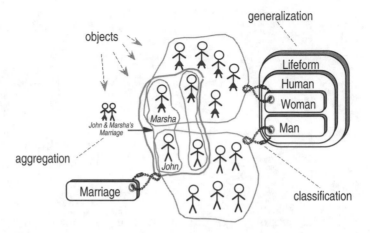

Figure 13.5.   Classification, generalization, and aggregation.

Classification removes certain distinctions, so that we can see commonalities between objects. Without classification, we would only know that everything is different. With classification, we reduce complexity by forming object types. Classification, then, defines a relation between object types and their instances.

The second mechanism is *generalization.* Generalization distinguishes a object type that is more encompassing than another. It enables us to say that all instances of a specific object type are also instances of a more general object type—but not necessarily the other way around. With generalization, we can build hierarchies (lattices) of object types, forming more and more general object types. The opposite of generalization is *specialization.* Generalization, then, is not classification—but a *comparison* of classifications.

The last mechanism is *aggregation.* Aggregation forms an object configured from its component parts. It allows certain components of an object to change over time yet defines other components to remain immutable. It reduces complexity by treating many objects as one object. Aggregation is not a classification, although its configuration is expressed in terms of classifications. In other words, aggregation specifies the *types* of objects that consist of other *types* of objects.

In summary, classification can be described as an *instance of* association ("That object is *an instance of* Person.") and generalization as a *subtype of* association ("Woman is a *subtype of* Person."). Aggregation can be described as a *consists of* association ("John & Marsha's Marriage object *consists of* the objects, John and Marsha.") As Fig. 13.5 indicates, we can and do employ these mechanisms separately or together. There is nothing magic or mighty about these mechanisms. At their heart, classification, generalization, and aggregation are just relations involving object types and the objects. Furthermore, we can model these relations as we would any other relation. We may, however, express these relations with special symbols, because they are so commonly used.

REFERENCES

Abiteboul, Serge and Richard Hull, "IFO: A Formal Semantic Database Model," *ACM Transactions on Database Systems,* 12:4, December 1987, pp. 525–565.

Bolton, Neil, *Conceptual Formation,* Pergamon Press, Oxford, 1977.

Borgida, Alexander T. et al., "Generalization/Specialization as a Basis for Software Specification," *On Conceptual Modelling,* Michael L. Brodie et al. eds., Springer-Verlag, New York, 1984, pp. 87–117.

Brodie, M. L. and D. Ridjanovic, "On the Design and Specification of Database Transactions," *On Conceptual Modelling: Perspectives from Artificial Intelligence, Databases, and Programming Languages,* Michael L. Brodie et al. eds., Springer-Verlag, New York, 1984, pp. 277–312.

Daintith, John and R. D. Nelson, eds., *Dictionary of Mathematics,* Penguin Books, London, 1989.

Flew, Anthony, *A Dictionary of Philosophy,* (2nd revised edition), Macmillan Press, London, 1984.

Langer, Susanne K., *An Introduction to Symbolic Logic,* (3rd edition), Dover Publications, New York, 1967.

Smith, John M. and Diane C. P. Smith, "Database Classifications: Aggregation and Generalization," *ACM Transactions on Database Systems,* 2:2, June 1977, pp. 105–113.

Part V
Object Aggregation

Aggregation is a reasonably new way of thinking for system developers. There was always the notion of "consists of," but it was not well understood or well implemented. The first article, *Six Different Kinds of Aggregation*, provides an overview of the various forms of aggregation. In particular, it describes the part-whole relation and the ways in which we think about and use part-whole situations.

The remaining two columns describe a logical foundation for modeling those object types and relationships that have an internal part-whole structure. For example, a car is composed of its engine, wheels, and so on. Furthermore, the car's aggregation has an internal structure that defines the way its parts are connected. Expressing aggregation, then, implies that objects can consist of other objects as well as specifying the interconnected structure of component objects. No object-oriented languages currently implement aggregation directly as described in these two papers. However, as people and system developers, we tend to employ these three techniques (classification, generalization and aggregation) all the time. The articles, *Foundation for Aggregation* and *A User-Level Model of Aggregation,* are contained here to bring more science to the art of aggregation.

Six Different Kinds of Aggregation

January 1994

Aggregation is a mechanism for forming an object *whole* using other objects as its *parts.* It reduces complexity by treating many objects as one object. This article examines the ways in which we form these whole-part associations by answering the following questions:

- What are the primary kinds of aggregation relationships?
- What kinds of relationships are often confused with aggregation relationships?
- How do these various kinds of relationships help us to make correct inferences about whole-part associations?
- How will these various kinds of aggregation help us during system development?

KINDS OF AGGREGATION

Linguistics, logic, and cognitive psychology have focused on understanding the nature of relationships. One important type of relationship is the association between the parts of things and the wholes they make up. In a joint paper, Morton Winston, Roger Chaffin, and Douglas Herrmann [Winston, 1987] discussed various expressions of the whole-part association:

> "The X is part of the Y," "X is partly Y," "Xs are part of Ys," "X is a part of Y," "The parts of a Y include the Xs, the Zs. . . ," and similar expressions, such as the sentences: "The head is part of the body"; "Bicycles are

partly aluminum"; "Pistons are parts of engines"; "Dating is part of ado-
lescence"; "The parts of a flower include the stamen, the petals, etc. . . ."
We will refer to [such] relationships . . . as "meronymic" relations after the
Greek *meros* for part.

Winston et al. describe several kinds of *aggregation* (or *meronymic*) relationships. The kind of relationship is determined by the combination of
three basic properties:

- Configuration—whether or not the parts bear a particular functional or structural relationship to one another or to the object they
  constitute.
- Homeomerous—whether or not the parts are the same kind of
  thing as the whole.
- Invariance—whether or not the parts can be separated from the
  whole.

This article presents six kinds of aggregation based on particular combinations of these three basic properties. (A matrix illustrating this is presented
at the end of this section.) The six combinations provide a reasonable guide
to employing whole-part relationships.

Component-Integral Object Aggregation

The most common form of aggregation is the component-integral object
relationship.

> A *component-integral object* aggregation relationship defines
> a configuration of parts within a whole.

To be a configuration, the parts are required to bear a particular functional or structural relationship to one another—as well as to the object they constitute. Some examples of this are the following

- Bristles are part of a toothbrush.
- Wheels are part of a grocery cart.
- Scenes are parts of films.
- Projective geometry is part of mathematics.

In this form of aggregation, an *integral object* is divided into *component* parts—which are objects in their own right. Here, the components cannot be haphazardly arranged. Instead, they must bear a particular relationship to one another and to the whole they constitute. The integral object, therefore, is a whole that exhibits a patterned structure or organization. For example, musical pieces or theatrical productions have a patterned organization. We refer to "the flute part" in a woodwind quintet or a "part" in a play. Such *parts* are components of an integral object. Objects in this relationship, then, can be tangible (toothbrushes or carts), abstract (mathematics or jokes), organizational (the EU or U.S. Supreme Court), or temporal (a film showing or musical performance).

However, when a component ceases to support the overall pattern of an object, a different kind of association results. For example, if a handle were ripped from the door of a car, the handle would no longer be considered part of the car. It could, however, be considered a *piece* of the car. Unlike components, pieces do not participate in the overall pattern of the object. They provide no functional support for the whole and typically have arbitrary boundaries.

Material-Object Aggregation

In component-integral object relationships, parts can be removed. (In UML, this kind of aggregation is called *composition*.) In material-object aggregation they cannot.

> A *material-object* aggregation relationship defines an invariant configuration of parts within a whole.

Material-object relationships are usually expressed in terms of the word *partly*. A few examples are the following

- A cappuccino is partly milk.
- A car is partly iron.
- Bread is partly flour.

Component-integral object relationships define the parts of objects. Material-object relationships define what objects are *made* of. For example, the component-integral object relationship would specify that a car has clearly identifiable parts such as an engine and wheels. The material-object relationship would specify that a car is made of such materials as iron or that bread is made up of such ingredients as flour. Components, then, can be physically separated from an object because their relationship to the whole is extrinsic. For instance, a kitchen without a microwave oven is still a kitchen. However, a loaf of bread without flour is not bread. With material-object relationships, the relationship between the parts is no longer known once they become part of the whole.

The word *partly* is not a requirement of the material-object relationship. For instance, a windshield could be made entirely of glass—not just partly. Other material-object relationships require a subjective judgment. For example, can the ceramics (of the spark plugs) be removed from a car? If so, ceramics is a component-integral object relationship, instead.

Portion-Object Aggregation

The relationships presented above define a configuration of parts that are different from each other and the whole they compose. In the *portion-object* relationship, the parts are homeomeric, that is, the parts are the same kind of thing as the whole.

> A *portion-object* aggregation relationship defines a homeomeric configuration of parts within a whole.

A few examples of portion-object relationships are the following

- A slice of bread is a portion of a loaf of bread.
- This chunk is part of my Jell-O.
- A meter is part of a kilometer.

Each portion or slice of bread is considered to be bread. Each slice is similar to other slices in the loaf—as well as to the loaf itself. The parts in a component-object relationship are not required to be similar in this way. For instance, an engine is not similar to the car of which it is part and is not similar to any other part of a car. On the other hand, a sip of coffee is coffee.

Portions of objects can be divided by means of standard measures, such as inches, millimeters, liters, hours, parsecs, and so on. Therefore, a meter is part of a kilometer or an hour is part of a day. In this way, the portion-object relationship is important for the arithmetic operations of addition, subtraction, multiplication, and division.

The similarity between a portion and its whole permits us to use a form of selective inheritance of properties during implementation. For example, the kinds of ingredients in a loaf of bread are the same as its portions. However, the *quantity* of ingredients for the loaf is not identical for each portion. The component-integral object relationship also permits certain properties of the whole to apply to the parts. For instance, the velocity of a car can also be implied as the velocity of its parts. However, since portions are similar to the whole, many more implications can be made.

Other terms that are often used in place of portion are slice, helping, segment, lump, or drop. The word *piece* is also used. However, care must be taken to ensure that all of the pieces are similar in nature. While the pieces of a splattered tomato are tomato, the pieces of an exploded car are not car.

Place-Area Aggregation

In the portion-object relationship, each homeomeric piece is removable. In the *place-area* aggregation, the pieces cannot be removed. (Again, in UML, this kind of aggregation is called *composition*.)

> A *place-area* aggregation relationship defines a homeomeric and invariant configuration of parts within a whole.

A few examples are the following

- San Francisco is part of California.
- A peak is part of a mountain.
- The 50-yard line is part of a football field.

This kind of aggregation in a relationship is usually identified between places and particular locations within them. Like the portion-object relationship, all of the pieces are similar in nature. For instance, places in California—including San Francisco—are still California. However, in place-area relationships, the places cannot be separated from the area of which they are a part.

Member-Bunch Aggregation

In the aggregation relationships above, the parts bear a particular functional or structural relationship to one another or to the object they comprise. Member-bunch aggregation has no such requirement. The only requirement is that the parts are a member of a collection.

> A *member-bunch* aggregation relationship defines a collection of parts as a whole.

A few examples of member-bunch relationships are the following

- · A tree is part of a forest.
- An employee is part of a union.
- That ship is part of a fleet.

This form of aggregation should not be confused with the classification relationship. For example, the following are classification relationships: Jason is a monster and Christine is a car. With classification, the set of objects for a particular object type possesses the same properties. The member-bunch relationship is different—based on spatial proximity or social connection instead. For a shrub to be part of a garden implies a location near other plants. For an employee to be part of a union implies a social connection. For these two examples to be classification relationships would mean that every employee is a union and every shrub is a garden.

Member-Partnership Aggregation

Members in a *partnership* define an invariant form of member-bunch aggregation.

> A *member-partnership* aggregation relationship defines an invariant collection of parts as a whole.

A few examples of *member-partnership* relationships are the following

- Ginger and Fred are a waltz couple.
- Steven Fink is a managing partner in Fink and Josephson, attorneys at law.
- Stan Laurel is part of Laurel and Hardy.

Members in partnerships cannot be removed without destroying the partnership. For instance, if Ginger leaves Fred, the waltz couple no longer exists. If Stan Laurel is replaced with another person, a different partnership results.

Aggregation Relationships and their Properties

Table 14.1 illustrates the properties that apply to each of the six kinds of aggregation discussed above.

NONAGGREGATIONAL RELATIONSHIPS

In the above section, six kinds of relationships were presented that express aggregation. Aggregation, however, is easily confused with many other kinds of relationships, such as spatial inclusion, classification inclusion, attribution, attachment, and possession. These nonaggregational forms will be discussed in this section.

Topological Inclusion

Aggregation is often confused with containment or *topological inclusion*. Topological inclusion is the relationship between a container, an area, or a temporal duration and that which is contained. A few examples are

- The customer is in the store.
- Monument Valley is in Arizona and Utah.
- The meeting is in the afternoon.

Here, the subject is surrounded, though the subject is not part of the thing that surrounds it. Aggregation, too, has the notion of containment. For example, the lungs are surrounded by the body. Additionally, aggregation involves a connection between the part and the whole that goes beyond just spatial or temporal inclusion.

TABLE 14.1

	Configurational	Homeomeric	Invariant
Component-integral object	yes	no	no
Material-object	yes	no	yes
Portion-object	yes	yes	no
Place-area	yes	yes	yes
Member-bunch	no	no	no
Member-partnership	no	no	yes

Topological inclusion is most commonly confused with place-area aggregation. An example of a place-area aggregation is San Francisco is part of California. San Francisco is surrounded by California, just as Monument Valley is surrounded by Arizona and Utah. However, San Francisco is also part of California, because of an additional connection between the two—every part of San Francisco is also California. In contrast, *no* part of Monument Valley is Arizona or Utah, because it is part of the Navaho Indian Reservation.

Classification Inclusion

The extension of a concept is defined as the set of objects to which a concept applies. Therefore, we can say that *Moby Dick* is *part* of the set of objects to which the Book concept applies. However, we would not say that *Moby Dick* is part of a Book. Instead, we would say that *Moby Dick* is an *instance* of a Book. Therefore, *Moby Dick* has a classification relationship with Book, not a member-bunch relationship.

Classification relationships can be easily confused with member-bunch relationships. Both involve the membership of objects in a set of objects. However, the member-bunch relationship is determined by a spatial, temporal, or social connection. In contrast, the classification relationship is based on the idea that a common concept applies to each.

Attribution

The properties ascribed to an object can be confused with aggregation. For instance, a Lighthouse has such properties as height and weight. Therefore, height and weight can be considered as *part* of the properties of each Lighthouse. However, properties are not components of the object itself. Instead, they are mappings from the object to other objects. While each Lighthouse has height as a property, height is not part of a Lighthouse.

Attachment

Attachment of one object to another does not guarantee aggregation. For example, Toes are attached to Feet and they are also part of feet. However, while Earrings are attached to ears, they are not part of Ears. For attachment to specify a component-object relationship, the component must provide functional support for the whole. While Toes provide functional support for the Foot, Earrings do not provide functional support for the Ear.

Ownership

Finally, ownership is often confused with aggregation. For example, it is true that a Bicycle has Wheels and that the Wheels are part of the Bicycle. However, while it may be true to say that the Girl Betty has a Bicycle, saying that the Bicycle is part of Betty is not true.

THE TRANSITIVITY PROBLEM IN AGGREGATION

A relationship is considered transitive if: whenever A relates to B and B relates to C, then A relates to C in the same manner. When relationships are transitive, valid syllogistic inferences can be made. An example of a syllogism is

premise 1a-	Socrates is a man
premise 1b-	All men are mortal
conclusion 1-	Socrates is mortal

Because this relationship is transitive, the conclusion can be correctly inferred from the premises. Aggregation relationships appear to be transitive such that: if A is part of B, and B is part of C, then A is part of C. In the following example, both premises are propositions based on the same component-integral object aggregation relationship:

premise 2a-	The engine is part of the car (component-integral object)
premise 2b-	The pistons are part of the engine (component-integral object)
conclusion 2-	The pistons are part of the car

However, keeping the *same kind* of aggregation relationship is an important factor in producing a valid aggregation-related conclusion. Even though the following syllogisms use only aggregation relationships in their premises, their conclusions are incorrect, because the *kinds* of aggregation relationship are different:

premise 3a-   Bob's arm is a component of Bob   (component-integral object)

premise 3b-   Bob is a member of the Math Department   (member-bunch)

conclusion 3?- Bob's arm is component/member of the Math Department

premise 4a-   The refrigerator is part of the kitchen   (component-integral object)

premise 4b-   The kitchen is part of the house   (place-area)

conclusion 4?- The refrigerator is part of the house

Just because the kind of relationship is different does not automatically imply that the conclusion will be incorrect. For instance, in the following example, even though premises 5a and 5b are different kinds of relationships, conclusion 5 is still correct.

premise 5a-   The loaf is partly flour   (material-object)

premise 5b-   A slice of bread is part of a loaf of bread   (portion-object)

conclusion 5- A slice of bread is partly flour

However, when the same kind of relationship is used, the conclusion is *always* correct. Aggregation is a transitive relationship. However, it is transitive only when the same *kind* of aggregation is used by the premises.

Knowing this fact is very useful when propagating operations on aggregation relationships. For instance, in a CAD/CAM application the user can request that a particular image of a car be rotated. Since the car is made up of many components, the rotation operation can be propagated to all parts of a car, as well. Since each component in the car can also have component-object relationships with other parts, these parts, too, can be rotated—and so on.

Another way of explaining this is by referring to premises 2a and 2b, above. Since both premises employ the same kind of aggregation relationship, the conclusion is correct. Therefore, since the pistons are truly part of the car, any operation applied to the car can be propagated to the pistons. However, with premises 3a and 3b this is not necessarily true. For example, giving a ten-percent pay raise to the Math Department could result in Bob getting a ten-percent raise.* However, since premise 3a is a different kind of aggregation relationship, Bob's arm is probably not a reasonable candidate for receiving a pay raise. Therefore, the number of aggregation levels that can be reliably propagated is based on whether the kind of aggregation relationship is the same. As long as this is true, the propagation can be inferred. If the kind of relationship is different, the application of propagation at each level must be examined for validity.

SUMMARY

Aggregation is a mechanism for forming an object *whole* using other objects as its parts. It reduces complexity by treating many objects as one object. This chapter examines six ways in which we form these whole-part associations. The six kinds of relationships are determined by combinations of three basic properties: configuration, homeomerism, and invariance.

These six kinds provide a reasonable guide to how we employ whole-part relationships. However, except for the member-bunch and member-partnership relations, they also help us to identify where aggregation is truly transitive and where it is not. As long as the kind of aggregation relationship remains the same, transitivity exists and propagation of operations can be inferred. If the kind of relationship is different, the application of propagation at each level is not guaranteed and must be examined for validity.

REFERENCES

Winston, Morton E., Roger Chaffin, and Douglas Herrmann, "A Taxonomy of Part-Whole Relations," *Cognitive Science,* 11, 1987, pp. 417–444.

---

* Note: this will only occur if the operation is expected to be propagated. Propagation is a property that is defined on an operation-by-operation basis. Giving a ten-percent raise might be chosen as *not* being propagated—in which case, neither Bob nor his arm would be guaranteed a ten-percent pay raise.

A Foundation for Aggregation

Conrad Bock and James J. Odell

October 1994

This column describes a logical foundation for modeling those object types and relationships that have an internal part-whole, that is, an *aggregational,* structure. For example, a car is composed of its engine, wheels, and so on. Furthermore, the car's aggregation has an internal structure that defines the way its parts are connected. Expressing aggregation, then, implies that objects can consist of other objects as well as specifying the interconnected structure of component objects.

A foundation for expressing the structure of composite objects is presented here. The computational services that can be derived from this foundation are also described. For example, instantiating the object type Car should create all parts of the Car and connect them according to the internal structure specified by the composite object type for Cars.

We propose a diagramming technique for composites based on these foundations—one which has better scaling properties than conventional representation techniques.

FOUNDATION

Qua-Types

Referring to a subtype that has been created solely because of a specialized relationship is often useful. For example, if a person is employed by an organization, the is employed by relationship can be expressed between the Person and Organization object types. However, a person who is employed by a company can also be specialized as a subtype of Person, called Employee. When an object type is subtyped solely due to such a relationship with another object type, the subtype can be referred to as a *qua-type* (or *qua-class* in KL-One terminology). It should be noted that qua-types are object types in their own right. The term qua-type is not a required term. Rather, it is a convenient way of referring to subtypes that are created solely due to a relationship with another object type.

Qua-Types in Aggregation

The aggregational relationship is one kind of relationship that can be used to create a qua-type. Composites sometimes require qua-types to use the same type of object in more than one role. For example, a car uses an engine to power the wheels; whereas, a submarine uses an engine to power the propeller. The object type Engine is subtyped into qua-types Car Engine and Submarine Engine to express more clearly how an engine is used in each situation. The powers relationship is restricted to relating Car Engine and Wheel (or Car Wheel) objects. Whereas for Submarine Engine, the restriction is Propeller. Without the qua-type, a sole connection to an Engine object type could cause confusion. In other words, an Engine would have relationships with both Wheels and Propellers—a situation which would probably not arise in the real world for a single instance of Engine.

In everyday language we frequently use the same word for both a type and its qua-type. For example, the qua-type is hidden when we say "a car has an engine," because there is a subtype of Engine that is peculiar to Cars. In other cases, the type is downplayed in favor of the qua-type. For example, "a company has employees" does not indicate that Employees are Persons. The distinction is drawn here so that there is no confusion in modeling.

Aggregational relationships are sometimes specialized, because two components are used differently within the same object type. For example, a car has four wheels, but only two receive power from the engine. The role Car Wheel is not fine grained enough to make this distinction, so the qua-type must apply to the specialized aggregational relationships Front Wheel and Back Wheel. The qua-type derived from this relationship, Car Front Wheel, can be powered by Car Engine, while Car Back Wheel cannot. (Assume for the sake of simplicity that cars are front-wheel drive.)

Composite Objects

Given the definitions above, a composite object type can be thought of as defining a collection of qua-types that are related to each other. For example, each Vehicle consists of such things as an Engine and Propelling Devices. Here an Engine has a Car Engine qua-type with a powers relationship to the Wheel qua-type, and a Submarine Engine qua-type with a powers relationship to the Propeller qua-type, and so on. The term *qua-type relationship,* then, refers to a relationship that connects two or more qua-types in a composite object. For instance, the powers relationship is a qua-type relationship between Submarine Engine and Propeller.

Composite Relationships

Once we have composite objects we generally want to connect them together. For example, when one Vehicle is towed by another Vehicle, we want the appropriate part of one vehicle attached to the appropriate part of the other vehicle. In this way, the towed by relationship could be composed of various attached to relationships, such as a Towing Connector is attached to Towing Bar, and so on.

SERVICES

Some services that can be provided for composites include the following.

Instantiating Composites

When a composite type is instantiated, it could be requested that all its components can also be instantiated—along with their appropriate relationships. For example, if a Car is instantiated, the Car Engine and Car Wheel can be instantiated as well. Furthermore, the powers relationship between Car Engine and Car Wheel can be established. In other words, a request to create a composite can also result in creating and relating all of the components. For composite relationships, the same situation exists. For example, when one Vehicle is declared to be towed by another Vehicle, the appropriate parts can also become attached to each other.

Propagating Composite Operations

One operation that is commonly propagated is deletion. When a composite instance is deleted, all part instances are also deleted. Other operations may also be propagated. For example, the rotate operation on a Car would be propagated to its parts. However, not every operation needs be propagated. For instance, painting a Car does not necessitate painting all its parts—only the external ones.

Maintaining Connections Between Parts

When a component is removed from a composite, it is no longer connected to the other parts either. For example, if you remove the engine from a car, it should no longer be connected to the wheels. Likewise, when you make the engine part of the car again, it should be connected to the wheels automatically.

Enforcing Invariant Aggregations

Sometimes a composite can consist of components that may not change. For instance, the Partners that are part of a Marriage may not be changed. Furthermore, if one Partner leaves, the Marriage is terminated. Here, the termination of a part results in termination of the whole.

Adding Components

When components are subtyped, additional types and qua-types can be created. For example, Race Car can be subtyped from Car, requiring additional parts such as Spoilers, and so on. Furthermore, the Engine object type might be qua-typed as a Race Engine.

Defining Composites from Existing Instances

An easy way to define a composite is to start with an existing set of inter-connected instances. With this service you select a collection of instances and their connections and get a composite object type that mimics its structure. In other words, you can instantiate the new composite type and get a copy of the original set of instances.

DIAGRAMS

If we try to diagram composites without using a shorthand for qua-types, the diagrams can become unwieldy. For example, Figure 15.1 shows a diagram using aggregational relationships along with ordinary relationships. (The unmarked lines are ordinary relationships.) The user is forced to diagram the qua-types explicitly. Engine is qua-typed for its different uses in Cars and Submarines. Axles are subtyped because only the front receives power in a Car. Wheels are then subtyped according to the Axle. Submarines use different Engines and are also qua-typed. The complexity of the diagram in this small example grows each time a new composite is expressed.

One technique for simplifying the diagram in Figure 15.1 is illustrated in Figures 15.2 and 15.3, where the user relates the parts as necessary

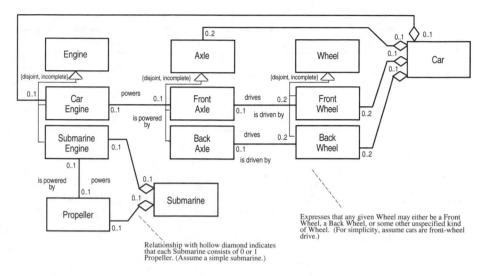

Figure 15.1.   Car and Submarine expressed with their qua-type components and qua-type relationships.

within the context of a Car or a Submarine. For example, Figure 15.2 depicts some of the basic parts required for a Car. The figure presents the qua-types not as rectangles but in parentheses above their respective super-types. For instance, while Engine is presented as a rectangle, its Car Engine qua-type is declared in parentheses above the Engine rectangle. In this context, the powers and drives relationships are assumed to associate the qua-types. Figure 15.3 employs this same technique for Submarine.

EXTENSIONS

Aggregation can be extended to include some other features.

Attribute Propagation

If a certain part of the composite should have a particular attribute, such as Owner, the same attribute would probably apply as well to the components. The composite object type can record this information so that instantiating Car will instantiate Engine and propagate the owner property to the Engine. Propagation is similar to the inheritance implemented for subtypes. It should be noted that not every property of a composite is propagated to its components. It must be defined on a property-by-property basis.

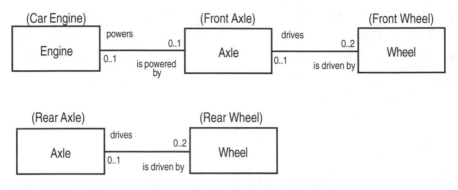

Figure 15.2. The components of a Car depicted with their qua-types annotated above their supertypes as a form of shorthand. In this context, the relationships associate the qua-types.

Partial Composite Instantiation

Since components can themselves have components, it is possible to create a large number of instances when instantiating a composite. For example, if you have a composite of a factory, you probably do not want to instantiate the enterprise down to the nuts and bolts. You can specify the number of levels down that you want to instantiate. Perhaps this can be further extended to indicate this on a component-by-component basis.

Ports

When creating a composite object type, you may want to limit which qua-types are available to make a composite relationship. For example, when connecting an engine to the rest of a car, you do not want the pistons connected to anything outside the engine. You can declare some qua-types to be *ports*—making them available to other composite relationships. For example, the spark plugs could be declared ports. The other qua-types can be considered internal.

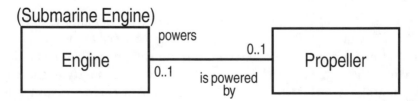

Figure 15.3. The components of a Submarine depicted with its qua-type annotated above its supertypes.

Implicit Composite Relationships

Frequently, the relationships between composite objects are idiosyncratic enough that they do not warrant a new relationship for each connection. For example, if you look at an electrical schematic, you will see ports on transistors connected directly to each other, rather than connections between entire transistors. The qua-types for the schematic are standardized (and therefore have a composite type for instantiation), but the relationships are not.

A User-Level Model of Aggregation

Conrad Bock and James J. Odell

May 1996

Most modelers express aggregation as a special kind of relationship between object types. However, when pressed to articulate how and why an aggregational relationship differs from a general relationship, a lot of hand waving results. In other words, aggregation often functions as a place holder for user intuitions that have not been articulated. Consequently, users have no common way to interpret aggregation when they see it on diagrams. This problem can be alleviated by showing how aggregation differs from other kinds of relationships. This column suggests

- A natural and useful way that users can think about aggregation
- Computational services that make sense from a aggregational viewpoint
- Development techniques, including a diagrammatic notation, that reflect the user viewpoint

A foundation for aggregation has already been published in JOOP [Bock/Odell, 1994]. (Portions of this foundation were also described in version 1.0 of the Unified Modeling Language [UML Partners, 1997].) Additionally, a taxonomy of aggregational forms was described by Odell [Martin, 1995]. This column balances these previous discussions by focusing on the user's model of aggregation.

USER MODEL

Aggregation is defined as a relationship that associates a whole and its parts, in which

- *Each part is of a certain type.* Each component of an object must be of some object type. For example, the component hierarchy expressed by an organizational chart consists of Organization Unit objects. The components of an Engine could be objects types such as Engine Block, Piston, and Crankshaft—or even just Engine Part objects. The way in which these part types relate may be specified in an object diagram (as in Figure 16.1) or via a Part Type hierarchy (where each Part Type may consist of 0, 1, or many other Part Types).
- *Parts may be connected in certain ways unique to the composite.* For example, an engine in a car powers the wheels, but an engine in a boat powers the propeller.
- *Each part has an identifiable role in the composite.* As indicated above, the same engine can be part of a car or a boat. When a given engine is part of a car, it is playing the role of a Car Engine; and when part of a boat, a Boat Engine. Each role can be thought of an object type in its own right—sometimes referred to as a *qua-type.* (A qua-type is a subtype created solely to support a role [Bock/Odell, 1994].)
- *Parts may be assigned properties unique to the composite.* For example, a Car Engine would convert its power in terms of miles per hour and a Boat Engine in terms of knots. For a Race Car Engine, you might wish to express the optimal ratio of the nitroglycerine required for the fuel mix, but not for the Family Car Engine.
- *Each kind of part may have more than one instance in the composite.* For example, a car may have four wheels.
- *Relationships may have parts or be parts themselves.* For example, when one person calls another on the telephone, the people are related by a composite relationship containing receivers, switches, wires, and the various connections.

Only the first and fifth of these features are in current methodologies, even though most of them are needed in common applications.

COMPUTATIONAL SERVICES

The following computational services are useful under this aggregational model:

Creation of Parts

When a composite object is instantiated, all the parts are created according to their assigned types and are linked together according to the connections in the composite model. For example, when a Car is created, an Engine object can be instantiated along with its associated Wheel object. The is powered by relationship is also established between the Engine and Wheel objects.

When a relationship is itself a composite, two or more objects are chosen to be related. Then, all the parts of the relationship are instantiated and connections established as for composite classes. In addition, connections are created from the newly instantiated parts to the original objects being related. Using the telephone example above, once two people are found for the relation, the various receivers, switches, and so on are instantiated and linked together. Finally, connections are made from some of the newly instantiated parts to the two people.

Destruction of Parts

When a composite instance is deleted, all the parts may be deleted along with their connections to each other. This is a special case of the propagation of operations, described below.

Maintenance of Connections

When a part is removed from a whole, it should be disconnected from the other parts. For example, removing an engine from a car disconnects it from the wheels.

Composite Inheritance

When a composite class is subtyped, its subtypes inherit the part structure of their supertypes. For example, the user of a GUI window might want to make a similar window with a few added controls. They can make a subclass of the composite class, which will inherit its composite model to the subclass. New part structures can be added to the subtyped window. Even when no parts are added, aspects of the existing parts may be restricted in the subtype. For example, trucks have engines because vehicles do, but they may be restricted to having heavy-duty engines.

Subtyping of Part Types

When a type of part is used in more than one composite, it may be connected to different things in each composite. For example, engines may be used in both cars and submarines. They power wheels in one case and a propeller in the other. How shall we model the Engine object type in this case? Two options are the following

- Since we do not know how engines will be used when we define the Engine object type, it is subtyped for cars and submarines—with the Powers association restricted to Wheel and Propeller, respectively.
- Make a Powerable Thing object type that is related to Engine and subtyped into Wheel and Propeller.

The advantage of the first is that it interoperates well with diagrams normally used to model object types, as illustrated in Fig. 16.1. The user can see on the diagram the constraints of exactly what connects to what. The disadvantage is that the context-based subtypes, called *qua-types,** increase the complexity of diagrams considerably.

The advantage of the second technique is that the diagrams are less complex. The user sees only that engines power some things shown as the subtypes of Powerable Thing. The disadvantage is that context-independent supertypes, such as Powerable Thing, need to be created for every connection of every reusable object.

Computational services can alleviate the difficulties of both alternatives: context-based subtypes or context-independent supertypes can be created automatically as the composite model is specified. The user can choose to hide them in the diagrams. The user can decide for each connection which technique to use.

Invariant Parts

Sometimes parts cannot be removed from a composite object without destroying the object. For example, a car may still be a car if its engine is removed, but not if its frame is removed. We are calling these parts *invariant.* When an invariant part is removed from a composite object, the object is deleted without deleting any other parts. For example, when the frame is removed from a car, the car object is deleted leaving the engine, wheels, and so on. Or, if one of the people who composes a marriage is removed, that marriage must also be deleted.

Propagation of Operations

An operation that applies to a composite instance may apply to all its parts. For example, this would include operations such as Move, Turn, and Sink. In

---

* Again, qua-types are subtypes that are added to support the extra functionality required for context-based properties—but not necessarily required by the user within the context [Bock/Odell, 1994].

other words, if the whole is moved, so are its parts. Parts deletion, above, is another example.

Accessibility of Internal Parts

When defining a composite, some of the parts may not be accessible for connection to the outside. For example, the pistons are not accessible to the outside of the car—only within the engine. However, the gas tank and brake pedal are. Parts, then, can be labeled to indicate whether or not they are accessible outside the composite.

Extending Inheritance

Composite classes with the above services are a natural extension of inheritance. Inheritance means a class can describe the attributes and operations of its instances, including those of its subtypes. Aggregation means that a class can describe the part structure of its instances, including those of its subtypes. Inheritance means that each newly created instance has its attributes and operations set up by the class, through constructors, memory allocation, and so on. Aggregation means that each newly created instance has its part structures set up, according to the composite model.

DIAGRAMS

If we try to diagram composites without using a shorthand for qua-types, the diagrams can become unwieldy. For example, Fig. 16.1 shows a diagram using aggregational relationships along with ordinary relationships. (The unmarked lines are ordinary relationships.) The user is forced to diagram the qua-types explicitly. Engine is qua-typed for its different uses in Cars and Submarines. Axles are subtyped because only the front receives power in a Car. Wheels are then subtyped according to the Axle. Submarines use different Engines and are also qua-typed. The complexity of the diagram in this small example grows each time a new composite is expressed.

One technique for simplifying the diagram in Fig. 16.1 is illustrated in Figs. 16.2 and 16.3, where the user relates the parts as necessary within the context of a Car or a Submarine. For example, Fig. 16.2 depicts some of the basic parts required for a Car. The figure presents the qua-types not as rectangles but in parentheses above their respective supertypes. For instance, while Engine is presented as a rectangle, its Car Engine qua-type is declared in parentheses above the Engine rectangle. In this context, the powers and

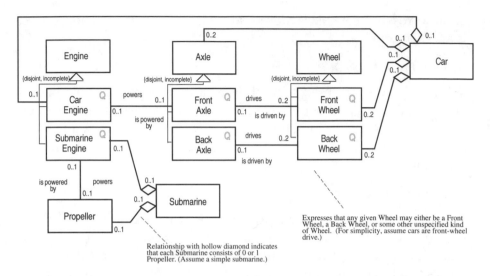

Figure 16.1.   Car and Submarine expressed with their qua-type components (marked with a Q).

drives relationships are assumed to associate the qua-types. Figure 16.3 employs this same technique for Submarine.

The diagramming technique in Fig. 16.3 presents aggregation without the specialized qua-types. Instead, the qua-type is indicated in parentheses above the object type that it specializes—reducing diagram complexity. A tool supporting aggregational diagrams can automatically make these notations as the types are added to the diagram. For example, when the user

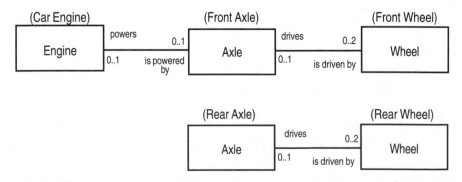

Figure 16.2.   The components of a Car depicted with their qua-types annotated above their supertypes as a form of shorthand. In this context, the relationships associate the qua-types.

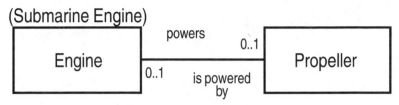

Figure 16.3.   The components of a Submarine depicted with its qua-type annotated above its supertypes.

asks to edit the aggregational structure of a Car, a diagrammer appears showing the part types and their connections. If the user adds a part by selecting a type, say Radio, the type appears with a notation indicating that the context is Car, where radios are installed in a way peculiar to Cars. Users can choose whether they want their part types to be automatically subtyped, as described in the section called Subtyping of Part Types. The tool can allow a aggregational diagram to be brought up from a normal object-type diagram, by a menu item to examine the composite structure of an object type.

The advantage of the above notation is that it indicates to the user that the aggregational structure resides in an object type. Thus, all of the type-based services are available, such as part instantiation, part-type subtyping, and inheritance of composite structure. The technique presented in the Unified Method [Booch, 1995] focuses the user on instances. This downplays the possibility of type-based services and may have resulted from the authors of the Unified Method wishing to simplify aggregational diagramming. Perhaps such an approach can be supplemented by notations or tool support that relate it to the type services.

REFERENCES

Bock, Conrad, and James J. Odell, "A Foundation for Composition," *Journal of Object-Oriented Programming,* 7:6, October 1994, pp. 10–14.

Martin, James, and James J. Odell, *Object-Oriented Methods: A Foundation,* Prentice-Hall, Englewood Cliffs, NJ, 1995.

Odell, James J., "Six Different Kinds of Composition," *Journal of Object-Oriented Programming,* 6:8, January 1994, pp. 10–15.

UML Partners, *Unified Method for Object-Oriented Development,* version 1.0, Rational Software Corporation, 13 January 1997.

Part VI
Design Templates

O bject-oriented code is typically generated in two ways. One is via an automated code generator that makes its own choices about how a given piece of specification is implemented. The other is via a manual code generator (i.e., a person) who makes her or his own choices about how a given piece of specification is implemented. But, how do we know that the generated code is efficient enough for the ultimate application? How can we bring some sort of guided consistency to the design process? Instead of having as many styles of reading a file as there are designers, wouldn't it be nice to have a "style sheet" that all designers use? In this way, maintaining the code would be much simpler, because a finite set of recommended and approved styles would provide both familiarity and predictability. These styles are called *design templates.*

These design templates* are formulated using a definition of both the analysis method and the implementation environment. In theory, the design templates are applied to the analysis model, and a fully working system can be produced. This system, then, will accurately reflect the analysis model, though the system may not be the most efficient.

The analysis model should *define the interface* of the software components. When used in conjunction with the analysis model, design templates suggest the *implementation* of those components. As a result, a programmer—new to the domain, but familiar with the templates—should recognize the interface of all the components simply by looking at the

---

* Templates are also referred to as *patterns.*

analysis model. While each template is a suggested implementation, its interface is dictated by the analysis model. (In practice, achieving this goal completely may not be possible, but aim to get as close as possible.)

The articles in this section take a number of analysis constructs and describe possible templates for each. Their description is provided in terms of both interface and suggested implementation. These general considerations and the sample templates should provide readers with enough guidance to develop templates for their own environments.

From Analysis to Design Using Templates, Part I

James J. Odell and Martin Fowler

March 1995

INTRODUCTION

In recent years, a movement has grown toward developing formal procedures to increase product quality. The work has been inspired by W. Edwards Deming who was sent to Japan after World War II to help rebuild their industry. His ideas on quality management, widely ignored in the United States, were taken up enthusiastically in Japan. Many consider this a key reason why Americans lost so much economic and technical ground to the Japanese.

This movement toward high-quality products, often led by defense agencies, has influenced software engineering. In particular, the work of the Software Engineering Institute (SEI) has proved deeply influential [Humphrey, 1989]. Their framework proposes five levels of process maturity: initial, repeatable, defined, managed, and optimizing.

The two lowest levels are the *initial* level (often referred to cynically as the chaotic level) and the *repeatable* level. While success in level 1 depends on the heroics and competence of individuals, project developers in level 2 can rely on established management policies and implementation procedures. These are based on the results of previous projects and demands of the current project. Developers meet schedules and budgets. Basic project standards are defined and followed. SEI studies have shown that the vast majority of organizations are at these bottom levels of process maturity.

This column provides an approach that will support organizations wishing to take a further step—up to the *defined* level. At the defined level, an organization standardizes both its system engineering and management activities. Such an organization exploits effective software-engineering practices when standardizing its activities. Furthermore, an organization's activity standards are tailored for each project to develop its own *defined* activities [Paulk, 1993]. One technique that supports defined-level organizations is *template-driven* design.

Template-Driven Design

In this approach, design activity focuses on forming a set of design templates that can implement the analysis model (see Fig. 17.1). These design templates are formulated using a definition of both the analysis method and the implementation environment. In theory, the design templates are applied to the analysis model, and a fully working system can be produced. This system, then, will accurately reflect the analysis model, though the system may not be the most efficient.

The analysis model should *define the interface* of the software components. When used in conjunction with the analysis model, design templates suggest the implementation of those components. As a result, a programmer—new to the domain, but familiar with the templates—should recognize the interface of all the components simply by looking at the analysis model. While each template is a suggested implementation, its interface is dictated by the analysis model. (In practice, achieving this goal completely may not be possible, but aim to get as close as possible.)

This approach enables both *consistency* and *traceability*. If a single set of design templates is used to develop code from the model, the resulting code will have a consistent style—a boon to maintenance and extension later on. This consistency comes from both naming the variables and operations and using the same mechanisms to implement bidirectional associations and subtyping. The link's directness eases tracing back from the code to the analysis model. Traceability is always useful and a key element for quality standards [ISO, 1987 and 1991].

Specifying Design Templates

The design templates can be specified in two ways. The first, and easiest, approach uses the design templates' document that has been adopted as a standard by a project or an organization. This document describes how to implement an analysis-level model for a particular implementation

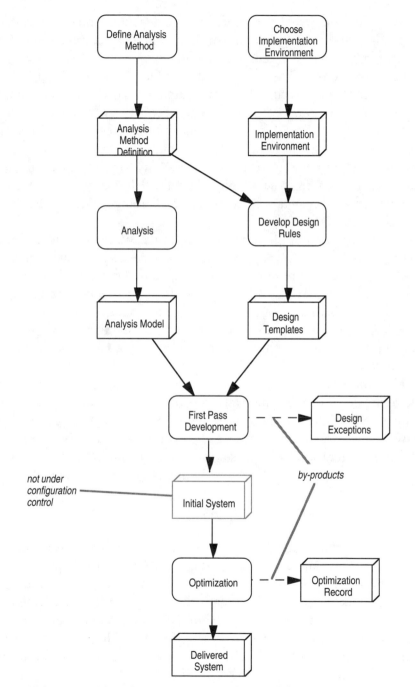

Figure 17.1.   An object-flow diagram which describes the process of template-driven design.

environment. Since the design templates are dependent on both the analysis approach and implementation environment, each combination of the two should have a design-template document.

The second approach encodes the design templates in a computer program. (This approach is currently very limited but is becoming more important.) Of course, this encoding is exactly what compilers and code generators do. A compiler merely uses a set of design templates to transform each kind of high-level language statement into binary code. Program-language compilers are not new. However, the technology to automate design templates is still very immature—though being developed rapidly. Code generators do exist that can take these models and produce much of the system code using templates.

This approach naturally has practical limits. While experience in formulating templates is growing, the idea of using design templates in this way is still fairly new. Furthermore, while design templates can be provided to cover most cases, they can not be applied to some special cases. Another practical limit is that the choice of design templates is not always well defined. Design-template documents may indicate preferred implementation options, while leaving the choice to the implementor on a case-by-case basis.

This column will take a number of analysis constructs and describe possible templates for each. The templates for associations will be discussed both in terms of interface and suggested implementation. (The next two articles will include such constructs as generalization and composition.) These general considerations and the sample template should provide readers with enough guidance to develop templates for their own environments.

TEMPLATES FOR ASSOCIATIONS

Associations—that is, relationship types and their mappings—specify how object types associate with one another. A number of OO practitioners are uncomfortable using associations in OO analysis, because they see associations as "violating encapsulation." Encapsulation dictates that the data structure of a class is hidden behind an interface of operations. For some, the presence of associations breaks this by making the data structure public. However, associations describe the responsibilities that objects must fulfill in their relationships with other objects.

For example, Fig. 17.2 specifies that each Employee object must be able to both know and change its employer. Conversely, each Organization must

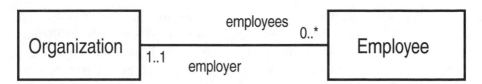

Figure 17.2.   Analysis models do not specify data structure. Here, each Organization has a mapping to some number of Employee objects. The employees mapping, then, is a property of Organization. To support this mapping, operations must certainly be implemented by the Organization class. However, a data structure may or may not be used to implement the mapping.

know its employees and be able to change them. In most OOPLs, this responsibility is implemented by retrieval and modification operations. Data structure may be present—and in most cases will be. However, data structure is a design consideration and is not specified by the analysis model.

Interface for Association Templates

For each association, the OOPL interface consists of a set of operations that access and update the association. The exact terms and structure of these operations depend on the cardinalities of the relevant mappings.

In general, a single-valued mapping requires two operations: an *accessor* and a *modifier*. The accessor operation returns the object to which a given object is mapped. The modifier operation changes the mapping for a given object by reassigning the mapping pointer from one object to another. Access requests, then, require no input parameters. Modification requests, however, require an input parameter that specifies the object to which the mapping must now point. Thus, for Fig. 17.2, the Employee class would have two operations. In C++, no standard naming convention exists. Here, many programmers use get or set somewhere in the name. For example, the names getEmployer and setEmployer (Organization org) could be used to access and modify the employer mapping. The names getEmployer and setEmployer are the most natural. However, some prefer employerSet and employerGet, because both operations will appear together in an alphabetically sorted browser. In Smalltalk, both operations are conventionally given the mapping name. Here, modifiers are distinguished from accessors by the presence of a parameter. Therefore, the Employee class would have get and set operations named employer and employer: anOrganization.

Multivalued mappings require three operations—again, with one accessor. Single-valued accessors return just one object. Multivalued accessors, however, return a set of objects. (All multivalued mappings are assumed to be sets unless otherwise indicated. The interface for non-sets will be different and is beyond the scope of this month's column.) Multivalued modifiers require two operations—one to add an object to a set, the other to remove an object. The accessor will usually be named in the same way that a single-valued mapping is named. However, a plural form is recommended to reinforce its multivalued nature—for example, employees or getEmployees. Modifiers would take the form of AddEmployee (Employee emp), RemoveEmployee (Employee emp), or employeeAdd: anEmployee, employeeRemove: anEmployee.

Modifiers, whether single-valued or multivalued, should also ensure that the constraints are met. For example, the SetEmployer operation should ensure that the employer mapping of Employee is not set to null. In other words, the modifier should ensure that both minimum and maximum cardinality constraints are met. Any other constraints, such as invariant, tree, and user-defined constraints, should also be enforced at this time.

Type checking should also be performed. For example, if a SetEmployer: anOrganization operation is requested, the object supplied via the anOrganization parameter must always be an Organization object. If type checking is not built into the programming language, extra code can be added to the modifier operations to ensure type integrity.

Association template option 1: using pointers in both directions

In this option, mappings are implemented by pointers from both participating classes. If a mapping is single valued, there is a single pointer from one object to another. For example in Fig. 17.3, each Employee has a single pointer to his employer. If a mapping is multivalued, the object will have a set of pointers to the other objects. In Fig. 17.3, NASA points to a set of pointers which, in turn, contains pointers to Peter, Jasper, and Paul. For languages that support *containment,* an object may hold its set of mapping pointers internally rather than point to an external collection. Containment, therefore, has implications for space requirements. Since pointer sets can dramatically increase in size, an object's size can swell. Single-valued mappings can also use containment. Here, the actual object will be stored internally, instead of a pointer to that object. Typically, single-valued containment is limited to storing fundamental objects internally, such as Integer or Date objects. (Fundamental objects will be discussed later in option 6.)

In option 1, the accessor operations are relatively straightforward. For a single-valued mapping, the accessor merely returns a reference to the

Organization   ◄ employer   **Employee**

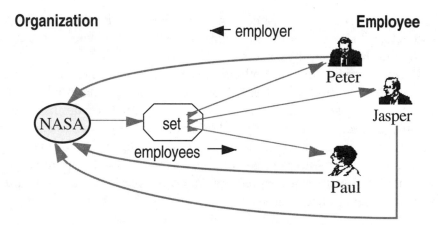

Figure 17.3.   Associations may be implemented using pointers in both directions.

mapped object.* For a multivalued mapping, the accessor returns a set of references. However, it should not return the *set* of references. If it did return the set, the set's user could change the set's membership—thereby violating encapsulation. The encapsulation boundary should include all sets implementing multivalued mappings. One solution is returning a copy of the set. Thus, if any alterations are made, they do not affect the actual mapping. However, this may incur a significant time overhead for large sets. An alternative is to use a *masking class.* A masking class is a simple class that has a single field containing the set. Only those operations that are permitted on the contained set are defined in the masking class. This way modifications can be blocked. Another alternative, particularly for C++ implementations, uses *iterators* as described by Gamma [Gamma, 1995]. Iterators provide a highly flexible way to access the elements of a multivalued mapping without exposing underlying representation.

Since two pointers implement each relationship, modifiers should maintain a two-way, or referential, integrity. Thus, a modifier called to change

---

* In C++, the issue about what should be returned by accessors is important. Should the object or a pointer to the object be returned? the choice should be made explicit by the design templates. A common convention is returning the value for all built-in data types such as String or Integer, the object for all fundamental classes such as Date and Currency, and a pointer for all other classes. In Smalltalk, this does not apply since it always *appears* to work with objects rather than pointers. This article will always refer to returning references. For C++ and other languages that are pointer explicit, the actual templates should make clear exactly what is being returned.

Peter's employer to IBM must not just change Peter's pointer to IBM. It must also delete the inverse pointer to Peter in NASA's employees' set and create one in IBM's employees' set.*

This template option has both benefits and drawbacks. Its accessor navigation is fast in both directions. However, ensuring referential integrity requires extra processing time. So, while this option provides fast access, modification requires extra time. Additionally, the technique to ensure referential integrity is not trivial. However, once a solution has been chosen, replication is easy. Another disadvantage lies in the space required for this option. Not only are pointers required in both directions, but multivalued mappings can require large sets.

Association template option 2: using pointers in one direction

Another option for association templates is using pointers in one direction only. In Fig. 17.4 for example, the Employee objects point to their employer Organizations. However, the inverse mappings are not implemented. Therefore, if all the employees for NASA are requested, a different method than option 1, above, is required. A common technique would be to read all instances of Employee—selecting only those whose employer is NASA. The containment approach described in option 1 can also be used here.

Without implemented pointers, accessors require more logic than the preceding template option. However, modifiers require less logic, because only the class with the pointer changes the pointer. The class without the pointer just requests the modifier operation in the other class. Referential integrity will not be violated when multiple pointers get out of step. This option requires less space than option 1, since it stores only one pointer per association. However, it will be slow when accessing objects to which there are no mapping pointers. So, compared to option 1, this option provides the same access time in one direction—but slower access in the other direction. Furthermore, this option requires less modification time and less pointer storage.

---

* Of course, care must be taken not to enter into an endless loop. Such as example would be where RemoveEmployee requests RemoveEmployer, which requests RemoveEmployee, and so on. In C++, this is a typical situation that requires a *friend* construct. In Smalltalk, a friend-like operation must be created—but marked private (which does not, of course, stop Employee from using it). In these cases, having only one modifier do the actual work is useful. The other modifier should then call just that one modifier. This will ensure that only one copy of the update code exits.

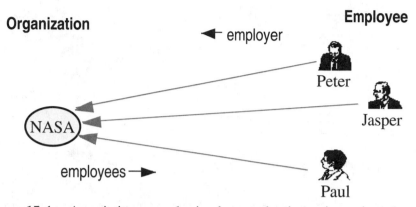

Figure 17.4.   Associations may be implemented using pointers in only one direction.

Association template option 3: using association objects

Association objects are objects with two pointers that are simply used to link two associated objects, as illustrated in Fig. 17.5. Typically, a table of such objects is provided for each association. Accessors work by retrieving all objects within that table, selecting those objects that point to the source, and then following each pointer to the mapped objects. Modification operations are simple. They merely create or delete the association object— thereby ensuring referential integrity without the two-way processing required in option 1. To support associations of this kind, special association classes can be built. Additionally, dictionary classes using hash-table lookups may be used to implement them.

Space is only used when associations are needed. This can be a benefit or drawback. When the objects of two classes are rarely related, few associations and less space are required. When the objects of two classes are usually related, more space is required. Furthermore, association objects provide slower access than previous options. Indexing them (by using a dictionary) can improve speed. One benefit of associations, however, is that referential integrity will not be violated. In addition, no modifications are required to the data structure of the two associated classes. In this way, any number association classes can be established or removed without having a structural impact on the associated classes.

Association template option 4: derived associations

Associations can be supported without any immediate data structure. For example in Fig. 17.6, the mother and father mappings will probably be imple-

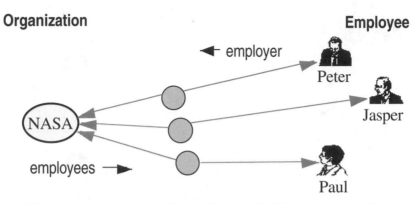

Figure 17.5.   Associations may be implemented with association objects.

mented with two fields that store the pointers to the Person's mother and father. However, the parents mapping does not require a data structure because it can be derived using the mother and father mappings. Mappings, such as parents, are usually derived in one of two ways—*eager* or *lazy.*

A lazy derivation produces its result only when a specific request is made. For instance, if the ancestors mapping were lazy, it would evaluate the ancestors only when a getAncestors request was issued. Implementing a data structure for a lazy association such as ancestors is not necessary. Lazy results are usually not stored within an object, because their results can quickly become obsolete between derivations. To ensure a derivation is always accurate and current, eager associations are used. An eager association derives its result whenever a change in one of its component mappings occurs. For instance, if the parents mapping were eager, it would calculate the parents in the unlikely event that the mother or father of a Person were changed. The product of eager derivations is typically stored in the object. Otherwise, the results of the derivation could be lost. In this situation, implementing a parents data structure is useful.

In this template option, the lazy accessor method involves more than following a pointer. It involves a method that eventually derives the pointer. The eager accessor, however, follows a pointer derived earlier by a modifier. Either way, the interface remains the same. The requestor does not know whether the getAncestors operation follows a pointer or performs a derivation. The requestor only needs to know that requesting the getAncestors operation returns a set of Person objects that are the ancestors of a given Person.

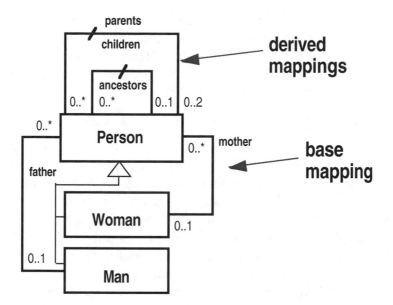

Figure 17.6.   An example of derived and base (i.e., underived) mappings.

Since the mapping is derived, modifier operations should not be available.* For instance, the ancestors mapping should not be modified directly. Any modification should be made to the mother and father mappings. If the ancestors mapping were lazy, any subsequent getAncestors operations would obtain the updated set of ancestors. If the ancestors mapping were eager, a modifier operation would have to be written to recompute and store the set of ancestors whenever mother and father mappings changed. Such a modifier should be invoked only from the setMother and setFather operations—and unavailable publicly.

Association template option 5: hybrid associations

Up to this point, associations have been implemented either as base or derived. Some applications may require that an association accommodate both modes. For instance, a particular ancestor of a Person may be known

---

* An exception to this is the *hybrid* mapping. Here, a mapping instance can be asserted or derived. For instance, a person's grandparents may be expressed explicitly, yet the great grandparents may be derived from the grandparents. This is particularly useful in those situations where the mother or father are unknown. Hybrid mappings, then, would require an appropriate data structure and modifier operation.

and explicitly asserted by an application. Yet, the remaining ancestors may still require derivation. In both cases, the ancestors mapping is a mapping from a given Person to the Person's ancestors. However, different methods are selected to access them. Here, the template option can involve a combination of option 4 and a preceding option.

Association template option 6: fundamental associations

Some object types are fairly simple and prevalent throughout all parts of a model. As such, they require slightly different treatment to most object types, particularly with respect to associations. Examples of such object types are the so-called *built-in* data types of programming environments, such as Integer, Real, String, and Date. Additionally, good OO analysis will uncover other examples of commonly used object types, such as Quantity, Money, Time Period, and Currency. The built-in data types, together with other commonly used types, comprise the *fundamental types.*

Fundamental types, then, are commonly used types and have a certain internal simplicity. Because of their common use, they will have many associations with other types. Mappings to a fundamental type are not a big concern. Mappings *from* a fundamental type require a large amount of pointer space and significant effort in maintaining referential integrity. This situation would also suggest a large number of accessors to support the queries indicated for these mappings. To avoid the possibility of highly bloated interfaces, the mappings of fundamental types to nonfundamental types are typically not implemented.

Fundamental types should be declared in some way. One method marks the object type as fundamental in the glossary. For many modelers, associations with fundamental types are also referred to as *attribute types.* Declaring a mapping to be an attribute type would be a good indication to the designer that the inverse mapping should not be implemented (as described in option 2).

REFERENCES

Gamma, Erich, Richard Helm, Ralph Johnson, and John Vlissides, *Design Patterns. Elements of Reusable Object-Oriented Software,* Addison-Wesley, Reading, MA, 1995.

Humphrey, W. S., *Managing the Software Process,* Addison-Wesley, Reading, MA, 1989.

ISO, *ISO 9001 Quality Systems—Model for quality assurance in design/development, production, installation and servicing,* International Organization for Standardization, Report ISO 9001-1987, 1987.

ISO, *ISO 9000-3 Quality management and quality assurance standards—Part 3: Guidelines for the application of ISO 9001 to the development, supply and maintenance of software,* International Organization for Standardization, Report ISO 9000–3:1991, 1991.

Paulk, Mark C., Bill Curtis, Mary Beth Chrissis, and Charles V. Webber, "Capability Maturity Model, Version 1.1," *IEEE Software,* 10:4, 1993, pp. 18–27.

From Analysis to Design Using Templates, Part II

James J. Odell and Martin Fowler

May 1995

In defining design templates, it is important to keep in mind the purposes of the templates.

- To ensure that the software is structured in the same way as the analysis models, as far as is practically possible.
- To provide a consistency within the software.
- To provide guidelines on constructing software so that knowledge is effectively propagated throughout the organization.

These guidelines give us an important principle. The design templates both *define the interface* of the software components and *suggest the implementation* of those components. A goal in the process should be that a programmer, new to the domain but familiar with the templates, should know what the interface of all the components is simply by looking at the analysis model. In practice it may not be possible to achieve the goal 100 percent, but we should aim to get as close to it as possible.

Design templates should thus provide a statement of the required interface and a number of suggested implementations. The interface is mandatory. However, programmers may choose the implementation from a suggested list or produce their own alternative. In other words, the class implementor may change the implementation but may not alter the interface. The user of the class should not need to know—or care—what implementation is chosen.

Since design templates are employed using analysis information, this means that the analysis model performs two roles: as a conceptual picture of the enterprise and as a specification of the software components. As these roles are very different, the analysis model cannot satisfy them both fully. Thus, some "impurities" will appear. The alternative to this is to keep separate models. However, the overhead of keeping multiple models up to date is costly and difficult.

The previous column explored association templates. This one takes a number of analysis constructs and describes possible templates for each. In particular, templates for generalization will be discussed.

IMPLEMENTING GENERALIZATION

One noticeable difference between OO and conventional modeling practices is the prominent use of generalization. While generalization has long been a part of many data-modeling approaches, it has been often seen as an advanced or specialized technique. The close relationship between generalization and the class inheritance of OO programming languages ensures a central place for it in OO analysis.

Many OO analysis approaches use *generalization* as an equivalent to *inheritance*. However, inheritance is just one of several ways to implement generalization. Other implementation forms are also required—particularly for those situations where objects may change their object type or be an instance of multiple object types. For instance, if a particular Employee object is changed from being a subtype of Staff to a subtype of Manager, this is known as dynamic classification. Or, if a particular object is both an instance of Property Owner and Employee, this is known as multiple classification [see Martin/Odell, 1995]. Such situations require more thought since conventional OO languages only support single, static classification. The approaches to implementing multiple and dynamic classification can also be used to reorganize inheritance structures and to implement generalization in environments that do not support inheritance.

The interface for generalization will be discussed at the end of this column.

Generalization template option 1: inheritance

In most OO approaches, the notions of *subtype* and *subclass* are synonymous. In other words, inheritance is the chosen method of implementing generalization. This provides the best form of implementation when such an implementation is possible. The interfaces for each object type are

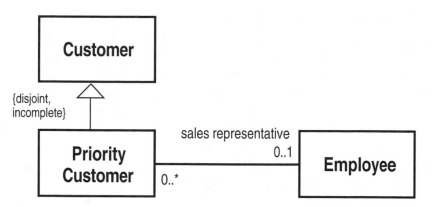

Figure 18.1. In most OOPLs, to change a Priority Customer to a Customer requires creating a Customer object, moving everything from the old Priority Customer object to the new Customer object, and deleting the old Priority Customer object.

placed on corresponding classes and method selection is supported directly by the OO programming language. Thus, this approach is usually preferred, if possible. Its disadvantages are that it does not support multiple or dynamic classification.

Generalization template option 2: creating a replacement object

One way to handle changes in object type is to employ inheritance as described in option 1. However, when an object changes in type, remove the old object and replace it with a new one of the appropriate class. For example in Fig. 18.1, if a Customer object becomes a Priority Customer object, the old Customer is deleted and a new Priority Customer is created. This allows the programmer to retain the advantages of inheritance and method selection while still providing dynamic classification. The full procedure for carrying this out is to

1. create the object in the new class,
2. copy over all common information from the old object to the new,
3. change all the references pointing to the old object to point to the new one,
4. finally delete the old object.

The biggest problem, in many environments, is finding all the references to the old object and moving them to the new one. Without memory management this may be nearly impossible. Any references that are not caught will be invalid *dangling* pointers and will lead to a crash that is difficult to debug. Thus, this approach is not recommended for C++. Languages with memory management can find this easier. Languages like Smalltalk make it even easier by supporting this option using the become operation.

Providing all references can be found and changed, this approach is plausible. Its remaining disadvantage is the time taken in copying common information and in finding and changing the references. This will vary considerably between environments and the amount of time required will determine the approach's suitability.

Generalization template option 3: flags

If a programmer who had never heard of inheritance was asked how she would implement Customer records to indicate whether they are priority or not she would probably answer: "with a status flag." This old-fashioned scheme is still effective for OOPLs as well, because it supports both multiple and dynamic classification. Flags are easily changed at will and one flag field can be defined for each subtype partition.

The principal difficulty with this approach is that it does not use inheritance. All operations and fields required to support subtypes, then, need to be moved to the supertype class. Thus, the Customer class in Fig. 18.1 implements both the Customer and the Priority Customer object types—resulting in an implementation like that depicted in Fig. 18.2. In other words, generalization is not being implemented using inheritance. Instead, it is being implemented using a flag field. In the case of Customer, the PriorityCustomer-Flag is a field in the Customer class.

If inheritance is not used, it is important to make sure that the proper operations are invoked. For example, it is clearly not appropriate to get or set the sales representative for a nonPriority Customer. If inheritance is used, such a request can cause an error (a run-time error in Smalltalk, probably caught at compile time in C++). Without inheritance, this template option must ensure that all operations originally defined on a subtype are guarded against incorrect usage. This is accomplished by checking the appropriate status flag to ensure that the correct kind of object is being accessed. For example, the getSalesRepresentative operation must make sure that the status flag indicates that the Customer object is a Priority Customer. If that check fails, the routine exits yielding some sign of the problem: usually an exception. One of the drawbacks to this approach is that it is not possible to catch this kind of error until run-time.

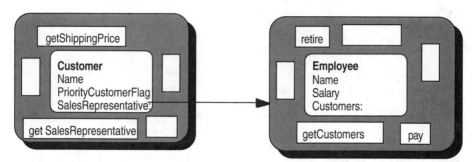

Figure 18.2. When inheritance is not used to implement the Priority Customer class, one option is to add a flag field and any Priority Customer-related data structure to the Customer class.

Since inheritance is lost, its partner polymorphism is also only a memory. For instance, if a getShippingPrice operation is polymorphic for Customer and Priority Customer, selection of the appropriate method needs to be implemented by a programmer. This is typically accomplished by using a CASE statement inside the Customer class. A single getShippingPrice operation is provided as part of Customer's interface. In the method for that operation, there must be a logical test based on the status flag of Customer—with possible calls to internal private methods. Providing the CASE statement is kept within the class and a single operation is published to the outside world all the advantages of polymorphism remain. Thus, the soul remains even if the body is absent.

The final disadvantage of this implementation is that the class must now allocate space for all the data structures defined for its usurped subclass. In the example above, this means that the data requirements for a Priority Customer must be supported within the Customer class. Thus, all Customer objects that are not Priority Customers effectively waste this space. If the subtype has many data structures—and few instances of the subtype—this is very wasteful, indeed.

Generalization template option 4: combination subclasses

Object types with multiple subtype partitions, such as depicted in Fig. 18.3(a), usually indicate the need for multiple classification. For instance, a given object may be both a Corporate Customer and a Priority Customer. One template option to support multiple classification is by using *combination* subclasses. This would involve creating classes for Priority Corporate Customer and Priority Personal Customer. By using multiple inheritance, the classes can neatly capture

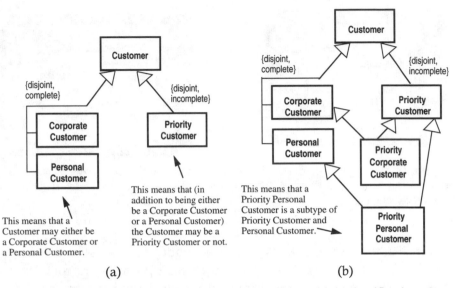

Figure 18.3.   Multiple subtype partitions (a) suggest multiple classification. One option to implement this is with combination classes (b).

all the required interfaces and let the programming system deal with method selection in the usual way. This approach is depicted in Fig. 18.3(b).

There are two principal disadvantages to this approach. The first is that an object type with many partitions could cause an unwieldy set of combination classes. For example, Customer could also be subtyped as Large Customer, Medium Customer, and Small Customer in one partition, and Government Sector Customer and Private-Sector Customer in another. Including the partitions in Fig. 18.3(a), this would involve at least 24 more classes to express all the possible combinations. The other disadvantage is that this approach only supports static classification.

Some C++ authorities advocate care in using multiple inheritance. In particular, it is a common convention to not allow common root classes in a multiple inheritance lattice. The diagram in Fig. 18.3(b) is one such example. Here, Customer is the superclass of PriorityCorporateCustomer through both PriorityCustomer and CorporateCustomer superclasses. The alternative is to only inherit from Customer for one partition and use the other partition as a mixin. A mixin is designed as an abstract class which is mixed into another class to form a multiply inherited subclass. In this example, CorporateCustomer could be defined as a subclass of Customer but have PriorityCustomer as a mixin. PriorityCustomer would not be a subclass of Customer. PriorityCorporateCustomer would then be a subclass of CorporateCustomer and PriorityCustomer, but would no longer inherit Customer from two different directions. Note that this is an implementation technique only. In analysis, it is perfectly acceptable for the PriorityCorporateCustomer type to be a subtype of Customer type via two supertypes.

Generalization template option 5: delegation to a hidden class

This template option uses *delegation* to handle the subtyping. Here, a class is defined for the subtype, but is hidden from all except its superclass. A field must be provided in the superclass for a reference to the subclass (which can double as a status flag). As with flags, all the operations of the subtype must be moved to the superclass's interface. However, the actual methods and data structure for the subtype remains in the hidden subclass. In this way, all requests are received by the superclass. Those requests that involve a hidden subclass are then passed on to the hidden subclass for the actual processing.

For example in Fig. 18.4, an executive employee would have two objects: one Employee object and the other Executive. The Executive object, and indeed its class, would not be seen by any class other than the Employee class. (In C++, all its members would be *private* and Employee its *friend*.) The give-Stock operation, defined only for Executive object, would be placed in the Employee class. When giveStock is sent to an Employee object with an associated Executive, the method in Employee for giveStock would merely call the give-Stock method in the Executive class. The Executive class would then return any result. In this way, no other part of the system would know how the subtype is implemented.

Note that this delegation is *hidden*. A common delegation approach is to make both classes public. In this situation there is no need to copy the operation definitions from Executive to Employee. The user of the classes is responsible for knowing that certain operations exist on the Executive rather than Employee. (This is often referred to as giving Employee the role of Executive.) This approach would not satisfy our requirement in this section that all the options share the same interface.

Method selection for polymorphic operations can be handled in a number of ways. One is to use a similar approach as with flags. Employee would contain a condition to check to see if the Executive field is null. If so it uses its usual implementation, if not it delegates the call to Executive. If Employee does not have the operation Employee raises an exception.

A different approach is to provide a separate hierarchy to handle the dynamic polymorphism. As illustrated in Fig. 18.5, the executive field (now

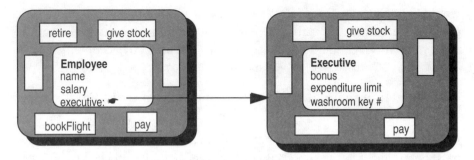

Figure 18.4. The Employee class with the Executive subtype implementation delegated to a hidden class.

renamed grading) refers to an abstract EmployeeGrading class, which is subclassed into concrete DefaultGrading and ExecutiveGrading classes. An employee who is not an executive would have this pointer set to a DefaultGrading whilst an executive would point to an ExecutiveGrading. The usual default implementation would be written into DefaultGrading and Employee would always delegate the call to the class in the grading field: no condition tests are required. This structure is rather more complicated than the prior paragraph but has the advantage that new gradings can be added without changing Employee. (This approach is described in more detail as the *state* pattern in [Gamma, 1995].)

The principal advantage of this option is the increase in modularity, particularly valuable if there are many hidden classes and the state pattern is used. In addition this approach does not waste space for those objects that do not need the extended data structure.

Generalization template option 6: object slicing

This template option is a more general form of the delegation option described, above. In order to support the dynamic and multiple classification requirements of a system, one recommended technique is called *object slicing*. In object slicing, an object with multiple classifications can be thought of as being sliced into multiple pieces. Each piece is then distributed to one of the object's various classes. For example in Fig. 18.6, the Sigourney object is depicted as an instance of the Employed Person and Property Owner classes. To record these two facts in a single classification OOPL, one piece of the Sigourney object must become an instance of Employed Person, and the other an instance of Property Owner.

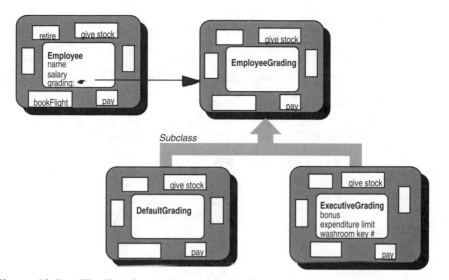

Figure 18.5.   The Employee class with the Executive subtype implementation delegated to a hidden class.

Obviously, objects cannot be "sliced" and made into instances of classes: it is a metaphor. These slices, however, can be implemented by surrogate objects. Each surrogate becomes an instance of a hidden class, as described in option 5. In addition, an unsliced version of the object must also be recorded to serve—physically and conceptually—as a unification point for its surrogates. Each original (unsliced) version of the object becomes an instance of some unhidden superclass called, for example, Conceptual Object. The instances of the other classes, such as Property Owner and Employed Person, are the object slices, where each is an instance of a different—but hidden— subclass. The instances of Conceptual Object are the unsliced objects, where each maintains pointers to its various slices, as described in option 5.

An example of how object slicing can be applied is illustrated in Fig. 18.6. In this figure, the unsliced Sigourney object is represented as an instance of the Conceptual Object class. This one object representing Sigourney as a whole points to multiple Sigourney object slices. The instances in the Property Owner and Employed Person classes are slices of the Sigourney object. In other words, object slices of the whole Sigourney object are also Sigourney objects. However, the slices comply with the conventional OOPL requirement that each is an instance of only one class.

Changes in state can be accomplished by adding or removing the surrogates and the pointers to them. For instance, when Sigourney was classified

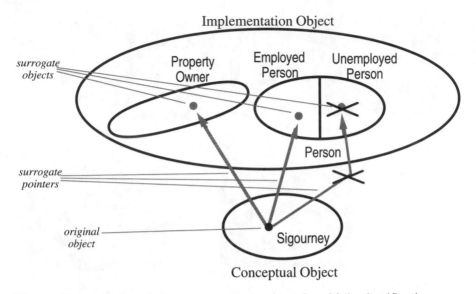

Implementation Object

surrogate objects

Property Owner

Employed Person

Unemployed Person

Person

surrogate pointers

original object

Sigourney

Conceptual Object

Figure 18.6.   Object slicing supports dynamic and multiple classification.

as Unemployed Person, there was a pointer from the Conceptual Object Sigourney to the Unemployed Person Sigourney surrogate. When Sigourney became employed, the surrogate Unemployed Person object and its pointer were removed, and replaced by a surrogate Employed Person Sigourney object and its pointer.

As each object is added or removed from the various classes, the Construct and Destruct operations would still apply. However, the object-slicing mechanism must add to these class-level operations by ensuring that objects do not have conflicting multiple states. For instance, an object can simultaneously be an instance of the Property Owner and Employed Person classes. However, it cannot simultaneously be an instance of both the Unemployed Person and Employed Person classes: it must be an instance of one or the other. In other words, an object cannot be classified as an Employed Person without first removing the object from the Unemployed Person class.

Object slicing is a reasonably elegant solution to a problem not yet well-supported by OOPLs. However, in addition to the programming overhead mentioned above, object slicing also requires extra logic to support polymorphism and supplement the OOPL's method-selection mechanism. This extra requirement is not used for those subtyping partitions declared as static. When a partition is static, the normal polymorphic support of the OOPL can be used. In this way, object slicing can be selectively applied. The developer must choose according the application's requirements.

Interface for Generalization Templates

Generalization, too, has its accessors and modifiers. Accessors return an object's classification, and modifiers change the classification.

A controversial question in OO programming is whether an operation *should* return an object's classification. It turns out that such an operation is often important. For example, without it how can a process take a set of Person objects and filter it so as to leave only the Women objects? Such an operation, however, also presents a danger: that programmers will use it within a CASE statement in such a way that subverts polymorphism. There seems little that can be done within the structure of OO programming to eliminate this dilemma. An operation that returns an object's classification is often necessary and thus should be provided. Good programming style, however, dictates that such an operation should not be used *instead* of polymorphism. As a general guideline, classification information should only be requested as a part of pure information gathering within a query or for interface display.

Some conventions currently exist for finding out the classification of an object. Both Smalltalk and C++ programmers use operations named isStateName to determine whether an object is in a certain state. Smalltalk has a message isKindOf: aClass to determine class membership. C++ does not hold class information at runtime. However, sometimes operations that effectively give this information are provided when a need is there.

Two broad naming schemes can be used. The first is to use the naming form isTypeName. The second is to provide a parametric operation such as hasType (TypeName t). The disadvantage of the former, more conventional, approach is that adding a subclass to the model forces a change in the superclass to provide the new isTypeName operation. The hasType convention is more extensible since subclasses can be added without a change to the superclass.

No naming standard exists for type changes. Names such as makeTypeName or classifyAsTypeName are reasonable. A general convention is that such operations are responsible for declassifying from any disjoint types. Thus a complete partition need only have as many modifiers as there are types in the partition. Incomplete partitions need some way to get to the incomplete state. This can either be done by providing declassifyAsTypeName methods for each object type in the partition or by providing a single declassify-

InPartitionName operation. Note that those partitions whose object types are invariant will not have these modifiers.

When these modifiers are used, associations will imply similar issues to those discussed under creation and deletion. Thus, mandatory mappings require arguments in a classification routine and a declassification routine might lead to choices akin to single and multiple deletion.

Implementing the hasType Operation

Each class in the system will need a hasType operation. The method will check the argument against all the types implemented by the class. If flags have been used, they are checked to test for the type. Even if no flags are present, the class will almost certainly implement a particular type and that type must be checked. If any of these tests are true, a value indicating "true" is returned. However, if none of the classes types match, the method on the superclass must be called and the result of that returned. If no super-type exists, "false" is returned. Thus, in practice a message sent to the bottom of a hierarchy will slowly bubble up the hierarchy until it hits a match— or it runs out at the top and comes back false. This mechanism makes it easy to extend the type hierarchy, because only the class that implements the type needs to check for that type.

REFERENCES

Gamma, Erich, Richard Helm, Ralph Johnson, and John Vlissides, *Design Patterns: Elements of Reusable Object-Oriented Software,* Addison-Wesley, Reading, MA, 1995.

Martin, James, and James J. Odell, *Object-Oriented Methods: A Foundation,* Prentice-Hall, Englewood Cliffs, NJ, 1995.

From Analysis to Design Using Templates, Part III

James J. Odell and Martin Fowler

September 1995

In the previous two columns, templates were explored. To review, design templates both *define the interface* of the software components and *suggest the implementation* of those components. A goal in the process should be that a programmer, new to the domain but familiar with the templates, should know what the interface of all the components is simply by looking at the analysis model. In practice it may not be possible to achieve the goal 100 percent, but we should aim to get as close to it as possible.

Design templates should thus provide a statement of the required interface and a number of suggested implementations. The interface is mandatory. However, programmers may either choose the implementation from a suggested list or produce their own alternative. In other words, the class implementor may change the implementation but may not alter the interface. The user of the class should not need to know—or care—what implementation is chosen.

In the previous two columns, association and generalization templates were explored. This column takes a number of analysis constructs and describes possible templates for each. Templates for creating, deleting, and deriving objects, as well as composition will be discussed.

TEMPLATES FOR COMPOSITION

Composition is just another kind of association. Therefore, the association templates described earlier can be used—with extension. Since operations may be propagated from a whole to its parts, the designer must ensure that the right operations are propagated. For instance, requesting a rotate operation on a Car object would also imply that the rotate operation applies to all parts of the Car. The owner field in the Car class could very well propagate to all of the parts, as well. However, requesting a paint operation on a Car object would not imply that the paint operation applies to all of the parts of the Car—only to the exterior parts. Furthermore, an exterior color field in the Car class would not apply to all its parts.

Since propagation is not yet directly supported by OO programming languages, a template is required to ensure that the proper code is in place. For those operations that are propagated, methods must be supplied for all of the appropriate parts. Furthermore, the method for the whole must ensure the methods for the parts are also invoked. The methods for the parts, however, might not be invoked unless the method for the whole is also invoked. For example, the move operation on a Car object would also imply that the move operation applies to all of the parts of the Car. Yet, you would probably not move the frame if you did not also move the Car. In other words, the move operation is not inherited: it is propagated, only.

In contrast, propagated fields do not have to be replicated to the parts. However, the part classes must have a method to access propagated fields— even if they are only contained in the whole class. In this sense, propagated fields can be thought of as being derived (as described the previous chapter under Association Option 4).

TEMPLATES FOR CREATING OBJECTS

Mechanisms are required to create new objects. This applies both to those objects implemented directly by a class and to those implemented indirectly.

Interface

Each class must have a way of creating instances of the types it implements. Creation does not imply just forming a new object. The various constraints that exist for the object must also be satisfied so that it is a "legal" object. All mandatory associations must be filled during the creation operation. This implies that the creation operation must have arguments for each mandatory mapping. Similarly, any subtypes in complete partitions implemented by the class must be chosen through arguments or the naming of the creation method. Additionally, invariant associations and object types should also be chosen through arguments.

Optional and changeable features *may* also be included in the creation arguments. However, it is usually better to create the object first and then send it the necessary messages to set up these features. This reduces the size of the interface for the class. While usually carried out by the class, object creation is not always done by the class. There are other ways to organize object creation. (See the creational patterns in Gamma et al.)

Template

All object-oriented languages have their own conventions for creating new objects. Typically, these provide for allocating the storage of an object and its fields. However, the initialization routine is not always an appropriate place for setting up the mandatory features passed via arguments.

In Smalltalk, the usual idiom is having each class support a creation message (often called new) which may take arguments. During creation, it is often arranged for the new object to be sent an initialize message that takes no arguments. This initialize is useful for setting the instance variables of multivalued mappings to a new set. However, it can not support initializing associations since it takes no arguments. Such work is best done in the new method.

C++ provides a constructor for initialization. Much may be done here but some compilers do make life difficult by not allowing this (or self in Smalltalk) to be used in an assignment within the constructor. Such a reference is necessary for associations implemented with references in both directions. In this case, a two-step creation is needed, using the constructor to allocate storage and a create routine to set up a legal object.

TEMPLATES FOR DELETING OBJECTS

Objects that can be created may also be destroyed.* The biggest problem in destroying objects is living with the consequences. Deleting an instance of Order, depicted in Fig. 19.1, would cause a problem if there were any Order Lines connected to it. As specified by the mandatory association, every Order Line must have an Order. So, if the Order were simply deleted, the associated Order Lines would violate cardinality constraints.

Two approaches can be taken to this problem. The first is the *single* destruction—the kinder, gentler approach. Here, if an object's deletion would cause any constraints to be violated, the destruction is not permitted. The second approach is the *multiple* delete. In this approach, if an object is

---

* Not all objects should be destroyed. Some objects, such as medical records, must live forever. Here, one alternative to destruction is archiving the object.

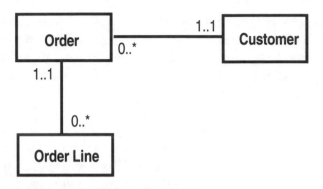

Figure 19.1.   Order objects may not be deleted when they have Order Item objects. Customer objects may not be deleted when they have Order objects.

deleted, any objects that require it are also deleted. For instance, if an Order were deleted, its Order Lines would also be deleted—causing a ripple effect throughout the database.

In practice, delete templates will vary from mapping to mapping, not from object type to object type. So, one mandatory mapping may only permit single deletes while another only permits multiple deletes—even though both mappings might associate the same object types. As long as the destruction is all or nothing, integrity is preserved.

Interface

Different object-oriented environments have their own approaches to destruction. All objects that may be destroyed should have a single-destruction operation. Technically, this is all a programmer needs. However, this places a burden on the user of the class to destroy things in the correct order. For example, to delete a Customer object, the programmer must also know that all Order objects for that Customer must first be destroyed. Furthermore, to delete all these Order objects, the Order Lines must first be destroyed.

Together with a single destroy, some multiple deletes may also be provided. It must be clear, however, which mappings permit multiple deletes, and which do not.

Template

During destruction, memory management is a very important issue. While it makes little difference to the destruction method itself, it does affect the consequences of error. The object being destroyed must have all its links broken with associated objects—*in both directions*. Additionally, all constraints must be checked for violation. Any violations that have already occurred due to the destruction operation must be rolled back. With a non-memory-managed system the final step is to deallocate the storage. With a memory-managed system, no explicit deallocation is made. Here, once all its links are removed, the object dies of loneliness and gets "garbage collected."

TEMPLATES FOR DERIVING OBJECTS

Returning a set of objects for a particular class is reasonably straightforward. However, the instances of some classes can be derived. For example, the Person object type in Fig. 19.2 has both derived and base (i.e., nonderived) subtypes. Employee is derived from those Person objects that are employed by an Organization. In contrast, Retired Person objects are not derived but must be explicitly classified as Retired Persons.

Derived classes are similar in nature to derived associations, discussed in Association Option 4 in the previous article. They can be lazy or eager. Such classes provide only accessor operations. For lazy classes, construct and destruct operations are not permitted, because derived objects are determined by criteria external to the class. Eager classes will have constructors and destructors. However, these operations should not be available as part of the public interface—only to those operations that implement derivation rules.

TEMPLATES FOR ENTRY POINTS

At this point, a well-designed structure exists of objects that are usefully connected together. From any kind of object, using the object diagram to decide how to navigate to any other kind of object is easy. However, there is still one important question. How do you get into the object structure in the first place? This may seem odd to those who use traditional and, in particular, relational databases, because the entry point to these databases is via their record types. Getting hold of the data involves starting at the record type and selecting individual records. Starting from a list of all instances of a type is not always the most appropriate approach. Object-oriented systems, in particular, can provide different forms of access which can be more efficient and provide other useful abilities.

The first way in which this can be done is to not provide lists of all instances for all types of object. Consider the example in Fig. 19.1. Since all instances of Order Line are connected to an instance of Order, there is no need to hold a reference from the type Order Line to all its instances. If it is

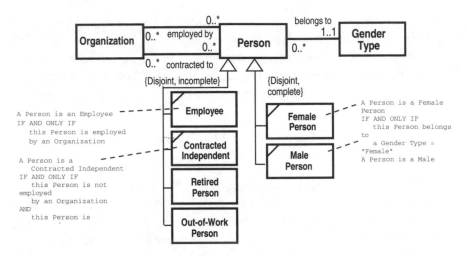

Figure 19.2.   An example of some base and derived subtypes of Person.

considered that it would be rare for anyone to ask for all Order Lines, regard-less of Order or Product, the reference can be neglected. In the unlikely occur-rence that someone would want a list of all Order Lines, this could be provided by getting a list of all instances of Order and navigating across the map-ping to Order Line. Thus, the storage required to hold all the references to all instances of Order Line can be saved at the cost of one level of indirection should all instances of Order Line ever be required. This is a purely imple-mentation trade-off. In a relational database, the trade-off is irrelevant since the database uses fixed tables.

The same argument can be extended to Order. Here it might be consid-ered that all instances of Order are required if a person wishes to select an Order by typing in an order number. Since the order number would typically be a String, references from string to Order would not usually be held. If an application required it, access to Order could certainly be provided by way of an order-number index. However, it might be argued that Orders were, in reality, always accessed once the Customer was found. In other words, ref-erences to Order could be obtained via the Customer object. Again, it is an implementation question as to whether to hold the references or not.

This argument cannot be extended to Customer since Customer lacks any mandatory relationships. Thus, a Customer can exist that is not related to any other object. A list of all instances of Customer is then necessary to ensure that such a Customer is found—making Customer a useful entry point.

Note that the decision of which object types should be entry points is purely a conceptual issue—not just an application requirements issue. Object types with no mandatory relationships must be entry points. Those with mandatory relationships may hold a list of instances, but that in itself does not make them conceptual entry points.

Interface

It is useful for all objects to have an operation that returns all instances of the type. This is essential for references in one direction to work when navigating against the grain.

It can often be useful to provide some operation to find an instance according to some criteria. An example might be findCustomer (customer-Number). While it is difficult to provide general rules, the most natural way is to use navigation. Thus, rather than asking to find all orders whose customer is ABC, it is conceptually easier to ask customer ABC for all its orders. Optimization problems may occur due to the navigational expression of the query, but these can often be resolved within Customer's accessor.

When access occurs using fundamental types, this option does not apply and a general find routine is more useful. Even then, it should be done in as general way as possible. The easiest approach is to ask for all instances of a class and then use the built-in select operation on the returned collection. This will not work very well for classes with many instances. The next move is to provide a select operation which will take any Boolean operation as argument. This allows maximum flexibility with only one operation on the class's interface. However, it is much harder to do in some languages than in others.* Only when these approaches are exhausted should a find with specific arguments be used. However, this should be done only when it is too expensive to do it in a more generic way. Care should always be taken not to bloat a class's interface.† Another reason for using a find operation is when a relational database is present. Here, the find operation would correspond to a SQL SELECT.

---

* It is easy in Smalltalk since the select operation can be invoked with an arbitrary block of code as an argument. In C++, a function has to be written which makes the whole thing a lot less elegant. One alternative is for each class to provide a general purpose find function which can be used to select instances. This can be called whenever collections of that class are needed.

† In C++, a common approach is to provide an external iterator and let the user of class loop through the selection manually. Although this is much more awkward than using Smalltalk's internal iterators, it is often better than using C++'s internal iterators [Gamma, 1995].

Note that these instance-finding operations would be as valid for non-entry points as they are for entry points. Indeed the instance accessors should fit the same pattern.

Entry points need an additional operation to make an object fit within the structure. Merely creating an object may not place it within the structure, particularly if it is not related to any other object within the structure. Thus, entry-point objects need an operation to insert them within the structure.

The above comments on interface are true for in-memory systems. Slightly different characteristics occur when using databases. Different data-management systems (either OODBMSs or relational interfaces) have their own conventions. Those conventions should be used with the proviso that interfaces be as free as possible of data-management system specifics.

Implementation

The usual way of implementing an entry point is through some collection class. This collection can be a static field for the class. Asking an object for its instances means that the objects of the collection are returned. As with multivalued associations, it is important that the collection cannot be changed except through the entry-point's interface. Another way is to have a manager class which looks after holding instances of entry-point classes. This class is usually a singleton class.

Typically, a nonentry point will also have an operation to return all instances. This can be done by navigating from an entry point. Selects and finds would work in a similar way.

REFERENCES

Gamma, Erich, Richard Helm, Ralph Johnson, and John Vlissides, *Design Patterns: Elements of Reusable Object-Oriented Software,* Addison-Wesley, Reading, MA, 1995.

Part VII
The Process of Objects

Many books offer their brand of how to design systems. The first arti-cle in this section indicates that there is not just one way to develop systems—there never has been nor will there ever be just one way. *Method Engineering* describes how to take the best from all approaches, yet be able to automatically customize a particular project's development process. More than 20 tools currently support method engineering.

User Workshop Techniques describes how to involve users effectively in the system-development process. Such collaboration avoids serial inter-views and potential misinterpretation of important information. The user workshop technique can be used for any situation which requires something more than a simple meeting or round table discussion—it requires a part-nership of management, end users, and I.S. professionals. Employing the user workshop technique has numerous qualitative and quantitative ben-efits. Providing a structured environment where key stakeholders can open-ly discuss important topics results in better and less costly systems.

Finally, this section provides an overview of how OO can be used to develop systems. *Object-Oriented Methodologies* describes how OO addresses a wider range of systems than previous approaches. The article concludes with an outline of the major steps that every methodology should address.

Method Engineering

November 1995

> A *methodology* is a body of methods employed by a discipline.
>
> A *method* is a procedure for attaining something.
>
> *Method engineering* is the coordinated and systematic approach to establishing work methods.

Traditional methodologies for information system (I.S.) development are—by nature—general purpose. As such, they contain an ideal set of methods, techniques, and guidelines that in reality can never be followed literally. They must be tuned to the situation at hand. Steps are sometimes omitted, added, or modified. Guidelines are often modified or ignored to fit special circumstances, such as technology, development expertise, the application, or external factors.

To complicate things further, numerous methodologies exist for I.S. development—each with its own set of tools and techniques. Comparing and selecting an approach from this methodological "jungle" is confusing and difficult. To aid in this selection, various comparison standards have been proposed for object-oriented methodologies, such as those documented by the OMG [Hutt, 1994a; 1994b]. Some approaches attempt to harmonize several methodologies—forming yet another rigid methodology [Coleman, 1994]. Other methodologies provide a choice of options, or *paths,* that the user can select depending on the circumstances. In short, an I.S. project can choose from three basic methodologies, as depicted in Fig. 20.1.

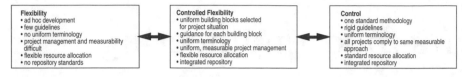

Figure 20.1. Methodological approaches fall into three categories (adapted from Harmsen [Harmsen, 1994]).

METHOD ENGINEERING

Flexibility without control can hardly be considered a methodology, since any systematic and coordinated approach to establishing work methods is absent. For such an approach to be systematic and coordinated requires method engineering.

Method engineering produces methodologies. For I.S., a methodology is a body of methods employed to develop automated systems. In turn, a method defines the steps needed to automate a system—along with the required techniques and tools and the anticipated products. Adapting a methodology to the needs of a particular project is sometimes called *situational method engineering.* For I.S., situational method engineering designs, constructs, and adapts I.S. development methods.

As indicated in Fig. 20.2, method engineering has various degrees of flexibility. These are as follows:

- *Use of a rigid methodology.* At one extreme, using a rigid methodology permits virtually no flexibility. Such methodologies are based on a single development philosophy and thus adopt fixed standards, procedures, and techniques. Project managers are typically not permitted to modify the methodology.
- *Selection from rigid methodologies.* Instead of permitting only one rigid approach, this option allows each project to choose its methodology from one of several rigid methodologies. This makes possible the selection of an approach that might be more appropriate for the project. However, this is a bit like buying a suit without having it altered. You make the best of what is available, despite the fact that the chosen methodology will probably not fit the project perfectly. Furthermore, each methodology involves additional purchase and training costs.

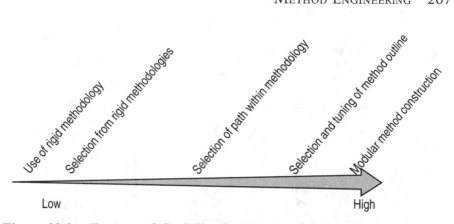

Figure 20.2. Degrees of flexibility for I.S. situational method engineering (adapted from Harmsen [Harmsen, 1994]).

- *Selection of paths within a methodology.* Many methodologies permit more flexibility by providing a choice of predefined paths within the methodology. Typical development paths include *traditional* and *rapid* application development. Some methodologies now include paths that support development aspects, such as package selection, pilot projects, client/server, realtime, knowledge-based systems, and object orientation. A common disadvantage, however, is that it may not be possible to combine some options. For instance, realtime, knowledge-based projects may not be supported.
- *Selection and tuning of a method outline.* This option permits each project to both select methods from different approaches and tune them to the project's needs. Typically, this involves selecting a global method process and data model. These models, then, are further adapted and refined by the project. This option is best supported by an automated tool.
- *Modular method construction.* One of the most flexible options is to generate a methodology for a given project from predefined building blocks. Each building block is a method fragment that is stored in a method base. Using rules, these building blocks are assembled based on a project's profile. The result is an effective, efficient, complete, and consistent methodology for the project.

   An automated tool is recommended for this option. Here, a project's methodology can be generated automatically and then adapted and further refined by the project manager. Performing the entire

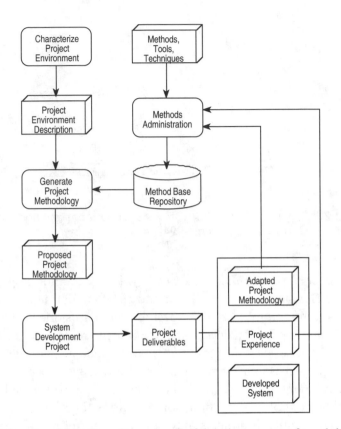

Figure 20.3.   An object-flow diagram specifying the process of modular method construction.

activity manually would require much work and time. Such an option is illustrated in Fig. 20.3.

COMPUTER-AIDED METHOD ENGINEERING

Computer-Aided Software Engineering (CASE) automates automation. In contrast, Computer-Aided Method Engineering (CAME) automates the assembly of methods. A CAME tool should support the following activities [Harmsen, 1994]:

- *Definition and evaluation of contingency rules and factors.* In order to choose the right method fragments for a project, rules and factors for selecting the proper method fragments must be defined. Method engineers are responsible for these definitions. Given the project profile and method base, the CAME tool selects and assembles the appropriate methodology.

- *Storage of method fragments.* Selecting and assembling a methodology from method fragments requires a *method base.* This method base is the repository from which method engineers and the CAME tool can select various method fragments. As new methodologies arise, they can also be incorporated into the method base.

- *Retrieval and composition of method fragments.* Certainly, for a CAME tool to generate a methodology from a method base, retrieval operations must be available for method fragments. However, total automation of methodology generation may never be completely feasible. A more realistic scenario could involve both automatic generation and a method engineer. The method engineer should be able to manipulate and modify method fragments within a methodology.

- *Validation and verification of the generated methodology.* The CAME tool should not only support selecting and assembling a methodology, it should also check the results. The tool, therefore, should incorporate guidelines to ensure that the correct set of method fragments has been selected. Furthermore, the tool should ensure that the fragments are assembled in a consistent manner. In other words, the CAME tool should ensure, or assist in ensuring, the quality of the generated methodology. (After all, generated methodologies must meet the same standards as standards methodologies.)

- *Adaptation of the generated methodology.* The method base should also accumulate the experience of previous projects and their methodologies. This experience should be used to improve method fragments, along with their contingency rules and factors. (Also illustrated in Fig. 20.4.) In other words, practical experience should be used to adapt future methodologies.

- *Integration with a meta-CASE tool.* CAME and CASE tools should eventually be integrated. When a methodology is generated for a particular project, the appropriate supporting tools should also be integrated. Adapting a CASE tool in this fashion would require configuring the CASE tool to support the resulting methodology. In other words, a meta-CASE tool would be required so that techniques and diagrammatic representations can be defined based on the methodology. Such a tool would be similar in nature to the

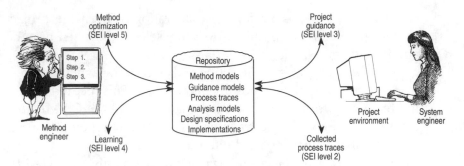

Figure 20.4.   An environment for process management.

CAME tool. Within this meta-CASE tool, CASE fragments would have to be defined. Additionally, it would require the ability to retrieve and compose new conceptual fragments.

• *Interface with a method base.* This method base is the repository for the various method fragments from which method engineers and the CAME tool can select.

To support CAME, the I.S. organization requires two additional roles—the *method engineer* and the *method administrator.* The method engineer is responsible for generating the right methodology for each project. The method administrator is responsible for the contents of the method base. Both support and are supported by the CAME tool—and are part of a larger framework called *process management.*

CAME tools are being developed by many organizations around the world. They are currently available from companies such as James Martin & Co. and Ernst & Young. While still in their infancy, the CAME tools from these two companies support many of the properties described above.

PROCESS MANAGEMENT

To support applications systems, the repository must—of course—contain information about the *product* of I.S. development. This includes information regarding analysis results, such as structural and behavioral models, business rules, and so on. For design and implementation, the repository would include information such as design templates, application data structures, programs, and interfaces. These kinds of information are indicated by the last three items depicted for the repository in Fig. 20.4.

Additionally, the development repository must also contain *process*-related information, such as intermediate results, human agents, tools involved, process plans, design decisions, and steps taken to execute them. These items are depicted in the top three items for the repository. These include

- *The method models*—containing not only the method fragments described earlier, but also a meta-model for handling the process-related information.
- *The guidance models*—guide the system engineer according to a recommended or enforced way of working. It also gives a structure by which process traces should be carried out.
- *The process traces*—track the various development components as they change during the system-development process. The guidance model describes the intended tracing. This portion of the repository contains the tracking instances.

SEI Support

The Software Engineering Institute (SEI) has been influential in the movement toward high-quality products. Its framework proposes five levels of process maturity: initial, repeatable, defined, managed, and optimizing [Paulk, 1993]. This same framework can be applied to process management.

Jarke recommends several kinds of SEI-related actions be performed that will ensure a high-quality process management environment [Jarke, 1994]. These are illustrated in Fig. 20.4. At the *initial* level, an organization does not provide a stable environment. Here, no repository exists. At the *repeatable* level, policies for managing a project and procedures to implement those policies are established. The planning and management of new projects is based on experience with similar projects. This is aided by capturing process traces, as indicated in the lower right of Fig. 20.4. At the *defined* level, an organization standardizes both its system engineering and management processes. Such an organization exploits effective software-engineering practices when standardizing its processes. Furthermore, an organization's process standards are tailored for each project to develop its own *defined* processes, as indicated in the upper right of Fig. 20.4. Once this has been established, the organization can introduce procedures for measuring the actual process execution. At this *managed* level, the organization learns to predict trends in processes and product quality. This action is depicted in the lower left of Fig. 20.4. Finally, at the *optimizing* level, the entire organization is focused on continuous process improvement (upper left of Fig. 20.4).

Method Models

Figure 20.3 illustrates how a method repository can be used to assemble the method fragments for a given project environment. To do this, the repository must include a method model containing the defined method fragments. If an organization prefers an *activity-driven* approach to defining its project environment, groupings of method fragments are selected to support a given kind of activity. For instance in problem-solving situations, a project methodology could be based on finding and executing a set of *actions* leading to a solution. However, many organizations prefer a *product-driven* approach that defines the deliverables, or *products,* first. The *actions* capable of producing these products are then identified.

Another approach suggested by Jarke is one that is *contextually driven* [Jarke, 1994]. Method engineers in this approach produce a methodology based on the project's situation and utilizing knowledge gained from previous situations. *Contexts,* then, are not only based on *situation,* but on *decisions* made in similar contexts. Additionally, the *arguments* that support or object to a particular context should also be available when generating a project's methodology. The meta-model depicted in Fig. 20.5 illustrates these concepts.

Guidance Models

As discussed earlier, a methodology is a body of methods. It specifies the route a system project will follow to transform the initial requirements into a final product that satisfies the quality criteria. Each of these methods is stored in a repository as a procedural module, called a *method fragment.* A methodology also prescribes the use of certain techniques and tools.

To generate a given project's methodology, a guidance mechanism is needed. The guidance mechanism is a pattern-matching engine. It matches products against situations in the repository. Once a match is found, the engine suggests decisions based on method fragment definitions. A guidance model, then, must support the mechanism by aiding the processes of decision making and problem solving and by supporting top-down or bottom-up approaches.

Process Traces

As mentioned earlier, traceability allows us to track the various development components as they change during the system-development process. Trace-

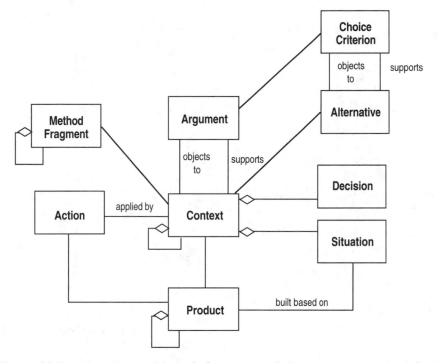

Figure 20.5. A meta-model depicting some of the concepts required for a process-management repository.

ability is important to the development process for many reasons [Ramesh, 1993]: support for product change and reuse; identifying critical require- ments and components; recording design rationale; project tracking and cost estimates; responsibility and accountability for fulfilling requirements; interdependencies between documents and components within and across life-cycle stages; and evaluation and improvement of methods.

During the course of a project, process traces are recorded about a vari- ety of things. The most common practice is to trace specification and rep- resentation changes. As illustrated in Fig. 20.6, the specification of a project's system often begins when it is little more than a vague idea. As the project progresses, the developers' understanding of the system increases and its requirements are recorded. The goal is to reach an agreement on the sys- tem's requirements and to specify these requirements completely. The process traces should record the various steps in producing the specification. Here, the tracking process should be tied to the methodology and the method fragments generated for the project. Since an agreed-upon specification

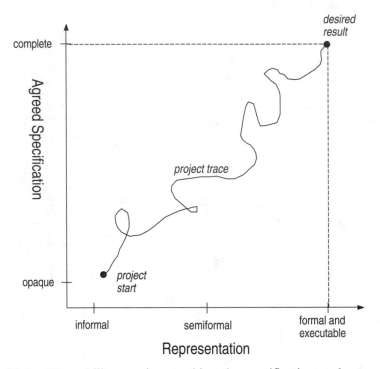

Figure 20.6. Traceability requires tracking the specification and representation path of a project.

requires consensus, the team should also track its progress in terms of choices, arguments, positions, issues, decisions, and revised decisions.

Each requirement in a specification will be represented in some manner. This representation can be informal such as prose or drawings. Or, it can be semiformal using modeling approaches, such as dataflow diagrams, functional decompositions, action diagrams, and entity/relationship diagrams. For any system to function, it must eventually be represented in a formal manner that is executable. This representation can be a programming language. It can also be some other formal representation that can produce an executable system, such as the rules, event diagrams, and object diagrams described by Odell [Martin, 1995]. The tracing process should track these various representations along with their connection to each other and to the agreed-upon specifications. Since many representations require consensus, the team should also track its progress of representation choices, arguments, and so on.

CAPE TOOLS

CAME tools are not available by themselves, but are part of a larger framework called *process management*. Such tools are known as CAPE tools (computer-aided process engineering). CAPE tools are being developed by many organizations around the world. As discussed above, CAPE tools automate and control the application-development processes, enabling the method engineer to develop fast, fluid, and flexible processes. These tools should increase planning, management, and development efficiency by providing tighter controls over each development project as it evolves. Furthermore, CAPE tools ensure that methods are designed to be reusable and can be continually revised and improved through integration of best practices from previous projects.

A CAPE tool is typically used for process management in four distinct modes—defining the process, planning the project, delivering the project, and improving the process.

- *Defining the process*—method components are created based on specific enterprise needs and characteristics. This ensures a successful foundation for a project. New method components can also be added to the library. The focus is on reusability and the intent that the processes will be used by project teams. This is also the stage where estimating elements are added and individual software tools are linked to method components as possible development mechanisms.
- *Planning the project*—project managers are assisted in planning by assembling the necessary methodology for a particular project. Since the method-base repository is constantly being improved from many different projects, project managers always have the most successful method components available to them. The methodology is tailored according to constraints of the individual project. For example, Fig. 20.7 depicts a "process filter" screen from James Martin & Company's CAPE tool called Architect. This screen helps Architect to select the appropriate method segments based on the objectives selected in the right side of the window. Once the methodology is generated, the project can be estimated and its risk assessed. Figure 20.8 depicts an Architect project metrics screen.
- *Delivering the project*—system development work assignments can be assigned to individuals and to development tools. CAPE tools can

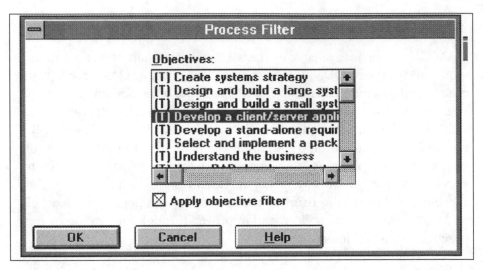

Figure 20.7. A screen that offers a choice of project objectives. Based on these objectives, the CAPE tool can generate an appropriate methodology (Architect, James Martin & Co.).

then guide the workflow of a project by ensuring that the right task is being completed by the right person, using the right tools.

- *Improving the process*—continuous improvement is key to process management. Using measurable quantitative feedback from each project, the method components used are re-evaluated to determine what worked and what did not. Here, method components are modified, added, or deleted to reflect the best practices and lessons from SDLC projects.

CONCLUSION

After all this, what does "method unification" mean? Does any one commercial approach have all the answers? Or, should we take bits and pieces of our favorite approaches and put them together in ways that make sense at a project level—in other words, start with "best practice" solutions and assemble them in ways that are appropriate for a project. This way avoids a "religious" battle over which methodology is the one true approach. Furthermore, there can be no "unified" approach—unless you mean that all the solutions are contained in a single method repository. The only measure of whether a resulting methodology is good or bad is whether it is *useful in a given context.*

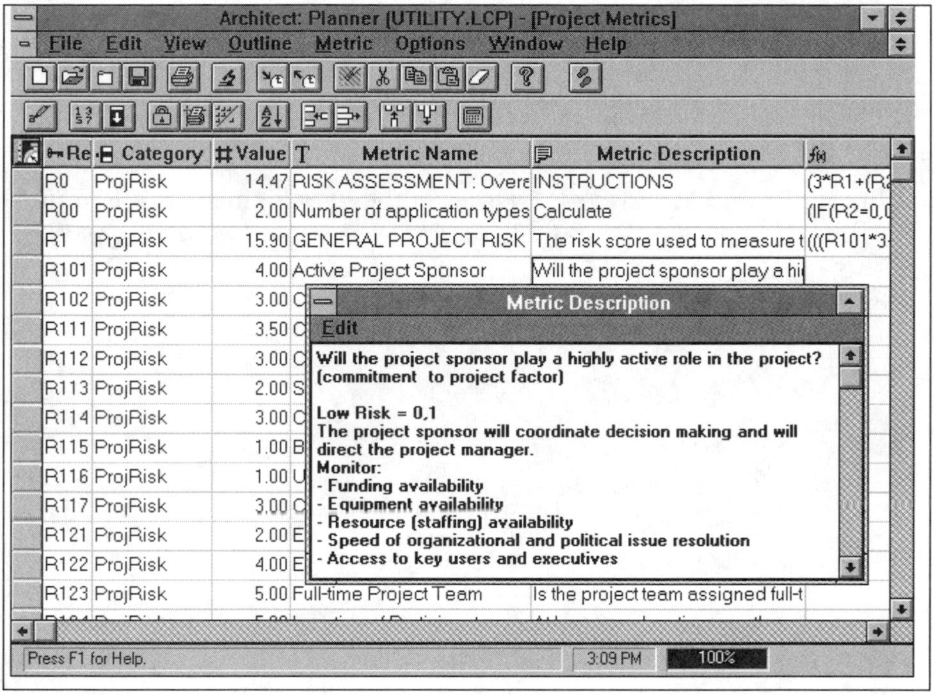

Figure 20.8. A screen that maintains and reports on various project metrics, such as duration and risk (Architect, James Martin & Co.).

REFERENCES

Coleman, Derek, Patrick Arnold, Stephanie Bodoff, Chris Dollin, Helena Gilchrist, Fiona Hayes, and Paul Jeremaes, *Object-Oriented Development: The Fusion Method,* Prentice-Hall, Englewood Cliffs, NJ, 1994.

Harmsen, Frank, Sjaak Brinkkember, and Han Oei, "Situational Method Engineering for Information System Project Approaches," *Methods and Associated Tools for the Information Systems Life Cycle,* A. A. Verrijn-Stuart and T. William Olle, eds., Elsevier, Amsterdam, 1994, pp. 169–194.

Hutt, Andrew T. F., ed., *Object-Oriented Analysis and Design: Comparison of Methods,* Wiley-QED, New York, 1994a.

Hutt, Andrew T. F., ed.,*Object-Oriented Analysis and Design: Description of Methods,* Wiley-QED, New York, 1994b.

Jarke, Matthias, Klaus Pohl, Colette Roland, and Jean-Roch Schmitt, "Experience-Based Method Evaluation and Improvement: A Process Modeling Approach," *Methods and Associated Tools for the Information*

Systems Life Cycle, A. A. Verrijn-Stuart and T. William Olle, eds., Elsevier, Amsterdam, 1994, pp. 1–27.

Paulk, Mark C., Bill Curtis, Mary Beth Chrissis, and Charles V. Webber, "Capability Maturity Model, Version 2.1," *IEEE Software,* 10:4, 1993, pp. 18–27.

Ramesh, B., and M. Edwards, "Issues in the Development of a Requirements Tracability Model," *Proc. IEEE Symp. Requirements Engineering,* San Diego, CA, 1993.

User Workshop
Techniques

July 1996

U ser workshops bring together the project's key people from both the business community (users) and the I.S. community at sessions facilitated by a professional moderator. Such collaboration avoids serial interviews and potential misinterpretation of important information. The user workshop technique can be used for any situation which requires something more than a simple meeting or round table discussion. User workshops require a partnership of management, end users, and I.S. professionals.

Employing the user workshop technique has numerous qualitative and quantitative benefits. Providing a structured environment where key stakeholders can openly discuss important topics results in improved decision making, ownership, and consensus, improved deliverable quality, more effective project teams, and reduced time and cost.

ROOM FACILITIES AND LAYOUT

The room should be large enough to contain the number of participants at a U-shaped table. Adequate walking room should be provided along with separate areas for a refreshment table, an observer's table, and breakout areas. Neither the participants nor the facilitators should feel cramped or closed in. Lighting should be variable for use with slides, overheads, and/or PC-screen image projection. Figure 21.1 shows the basic layout of a user workshop room.

Equipment

Appropriate equipment is needed in the rooms in which user workshops are conducted. Traditional items of equipment include

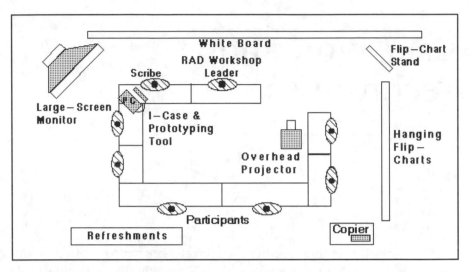

Figure 21.1.   A sample layout of a workshop room.

- One or more large white boards with dry erasable colored markers (printable white boards are preferred, if available).
- A kit for building diagrams and specially shaped blank magnets for modeling exercises.
- At least two flip charts with extra pads of paper, colored markers, and enough wall space to hang and display multiple flip-chart sheets. Lined or graph-paper sheets make it easier to write legibly. (More flip charts may be required if the group works in subteams during the workshop.)
- Stickers for structured exercises. Stickers come in multiple colors and large and small sizes. A stapler, scissors, paper clips, and related office equipment are usually included in the kit bag.

Computer items include the following

- PC with word processing, graphics, and software development tools. A large screen monitor or projector device helps all participants view the screens clearly and easily.
- Printer to provide participants with models, screen designs, and supporting materials.

Electronic items include the following

- Access to a copier (if not provided in the room) to produce copies of information created.

- Slide projector if the user workshop facilitator or executive owner has prepared slides.
- Videotape player and monitor if videotapes you plan to use video-tapes.
- Overhead projector and screen, transparency markers, prepared and blank transparencies. An extra projector bulb and enough electrical cords are helpful.
- Tape recorders and telephones should not be used. An instant camera may be useful for photographing white boards and flip charts.

Amenities include the following

- Separate refreshment table.
- Name card badges or tent cards for participants. Writing materials and markers may also be provided.

LOCATION AND DURATION

Location

User workshops are best held off-site—away from the normal work location of the business and system participants. Most hotels and conference centers provide facilities outfitted with the equipment listed above. Many enterprises have created JAD rooms, group decisions support centers, or facilitated workrooms which can also be used. If held on-site, take care to keep the participants from checking back with their desks to avoid group disintegration.

Duration

User workshops vary in their duration. Four-day or three-day sessions tend to be the most frequently used—allowing participants to have at least one day in the office or for traveling from a remote location. Complex system applications, or applications which cut across multiple business organizations (often where politics are of concern), may require multiple user workshop sessions.

Specific hours—Each workshop day should be typical business or working hours, such as 8:00 AM to 5:00 or 6:00 PM. Some sessions go late into the night, but common sense should be used when making these scheduling decisions. User workshops are intense events and participants' motivation and attitude has to be managed properly to maximize their usefulness.

Full and half-day sessions—Full day sessions are always preferred, but some cultures and availability constraints may dictate half-day sessions.

One advantage to half-day sessions is that the facilitator has time to prepare for the next session. Another advantage is that deliverables can be reviewed, modified, or produced by the scribe(s) and/or I.S. team. With half-day sessions, however, employing facilitation techniques for meeting management and behavior control is essential. Group effectiveness needs to be maintained.

Marathon sessions—Great results can be achieved in marathon sessions. However, experience shows that participants (and the facilitator) are not at their best the following morning. Client culture, level of participants, and type of user workshop will also affect the length of the workshop day.

USER WORKSHOP STRUCTURE

User workshops involve more than the time spent in the workshop sessions. Enough preparation time must be allocated before the workshop sessions to maximize their success. After the workshop sessions, finalize the documentation and prepare for the next step. The following three-stage model can be applied to any type of user workshop.

Preworkshop Activities

Preworkshop activities include

- planning and project scoping,
- research and background analysis (may include interviewing),
- executive owner identification and kick-off,
- participant selection, briefing, and training,
- logistical arrangements,
- selecting and preparing workshop exercises.

The facilitator will normally require two to five days of preparation time for each three-day session. Initial user-design sessions may require one to four days of preworkshop activity per five days of scheduled workshop time. Subsequent user-design workshops may require one to two days of additional preparation.

User Workshop Format

Each agenda will differ. However, all user workshops will have an opening module, a work module, and a closure module. The work module itself may be composed of submodules or structured activities depending on the topics to be addressed.

Postworkshop Follow-up

To ensure proper closure and to build ownership of the workshop results, follow-up should include

- deliverable finalization and validation checking,
- prototype extension (for design user workshops),
- expectation management,
- open issue resolution,
- executive commitment and decision to proceed.

Depending on particular responsibilities and assignments for deliverable construction and presentation, allow between one to three days of facilitator time for follow-up.

PARTICIPANT SELECTION AND PARTICIPATION

Selection

Participation should be full-time during the workshop—whether full-day or half-day sessions. Participants from the business community (users) should be selected based on their value and ability to contribute to the creation of workshop deliverables. The actual workshop should not be held until all the key participants are available. This may often require the executive owner to clear calendars/schedules to get the most knowledgeable users in the workshop.

Visiting participants may be allowed to attend the workshop as silent observers or as subject area experts. Subject experts may be part-time and only scheduled for certain workshop modules or activities.

Preparation

Participants should be briefed prior to attending a user workshop. Formal briefing meetings may be held in conjunction with kick-off meetings or separately. Any available materials pertinent to the project, such as a list of objectives or supporting documents, should be provided. Any existing models may also be distributed.

Participants should also be trained in all diagramming conventions that will be used during the user workshops. Example walk-throughs may be required depending on their familiarity with system development concepts.

Typically, only one half-day briefing session is required. Individual participants may be given assignments, if required for the workshop's success. Roles and responsibilities, objectives, and user workshop concepts should also be introduced. A formal briefing packet is typically distributed to all participants.

Kick-Off Meeting

Holding a formal *kick-off* meeting is one key to a successful user workshop. Whether or not the kick-off meeting is merged with a briefing and participant-training meeting, the meeting should be conducted several business days prior to the actual workshop (unless logistics and cost constraints are prohibitive).

The executive owner should open the meeting and then turn it over to the facilitator. The expectations of all participants, both users and systems professionals, must be established. Kick-off meetings should last no more than two hours. When combined with a participant briefing session, allow one full day.

Materials Assembly

A formal briefing book may be prepared and distributed to all participants at the briefing or kick-off sessions. Subsequent documentation or useful model extracts may also be prepared and distributed to participants prior to each subsequent workshop. Special packages should be assembled for the executive owner. Materials required to conduct user workshops, such as overheads, scripts, exercise walk-throughs, and/or strawman models, are the responsibility of the facilitator and scribe. These materials require preparation, reproduction, and possibly distribution time.

USER WORKSHOP AGENDA MODEL

Opening Module

Start-up items should be limited to 15 to 20 minutes. These include

- welcome remarks from project manager(s) and/or facilitator,
- housekeeping items (rest room locations, message system, smoking areas, and so on),
- schedule review,
- executive owner kick-off speech (optional, may be performed during preworkshop activities).

Prepare to Work

The steps for work preparation include the following

- Introduction to the user workshop technique and overview of the project's purpose and approach. Allow no more than 30 minutes.

- Review agenda and make changes as required (helps to establish rapport with group).
- Review and set rules of operation.
- Review the scope and objectives (that is, check expectations)—when the sessions start in the morning, resume after lunch, and close each day.
- Execute ice-breaker or start-up exercise (optional).

Work Module

The work module agenda is customized based on the type of user workshop, the particular objectives, and special client needs. Moderators should use facilitation techniques to manage the work items performed during this module. Keep to the schedule—but remain flexible for modifications.

Closure Module

At the end of each workshop day, allow a minimum of 15 minutes to accomplish the following:

- review agenda,
- summarize progress and modify as appropriate,
- elicit participant feedback and check expectations,
- always thank participants for their time and contribution.

At the end of each user workshop, allow at least one hour to bring closure:

- Always review objectives, goals, and agenda items.
- Summarize results to build up ownership.
- As an option, have the executive owner give a five minute closing wrap-up.
- Review open issues and check assignments.
- Prepare action plan.
- Evaluation and closure. (By current convention, a one or two page user-workshop evaluation form is distributed to all participants. Their comments are invaluable for improving the workshop technique.)

RULES OF OPERATION AND HANDLING OPEN ISSUES

Rules of Operation

This technique works best when the participants assist in determining how they would like to operate during the workshop. Normally the facilitator lists one or two suggested rules and then solicits additional rules. (It is often useful to think of all the bad meetings you have attended.) Then, consider what useful guidelines you would like employed to manage the meeting better. Some common rules follow

- Everyone participates equally.
- One conversation at a time.
- Critique ideas—avoid criticizing people.
- Five-minute rule for issue tabling.
- Observers only contribute when requested by a participant via a facilitator or break when participants break.
- Keep on time.

Handling Open Issues

User workshops should be well paced and move quickly. When an issue cannot be resolved within a reasonable time frame, it should be boarded for future resolution.

If there is a "five-minute" rule of operation, the facilitator and other participants need to invoke it when the discussion becomes bogged down or when an argument threatens progress. Issues can be either within or outside the scope of the workshop's objectives or project's scope. All issues should be written down for subsequent action.

- State the issue in a clear, concise statement or question. Check with participants for proper wording.
- Put the issue on a white board or flip chart. Keep an issues list posted around the room.
- For each issue list: issue number, issue statement, person assigned to resolve issue, date for resolution, suggested solution (if appropriate).
- Examine the issues list daily and at the close of the workshop.
- Rank issues for executive owner resolution or for a later workshop.

DOCUMENTATION CONVENTIONS

Deliverables are driven by the methodology, workshop objectives, and particular client needs. Typical documentation from user workshops should include

- list of objectives (project and/or system),

- system/application scope including preliminary (and final) list of system functionality,
- tangible and intangible benefits, return on investment,
- business model diagrams,
- user interface designs,
- interface to other systems,
- open issues list,
- implementation priorities, action plans, and target dates,
- executive summary.

Typically user workshops generate one to two days of documentation time for each eight to ten hour workshop day. Allow enough resources during and after the workshop to complete the documentation.

CRITICAL SUCCESS FACTORS

Critical factors affecting the success of the user workshop technique include

- executive commitment (resources, time, and people),
- skilled, experienced facilitator or session moderator,
- reasonable scope,
- the appropriate selection of full-time, committed participants,
- business focus,
- methodology concepts, principles, and conventions are followed,
- easily understandable diagramming conventions,
- proper environment and room layout/facilities/tools.

GUIDELINES

Contentious political issues may be known before the workshop. An executive owner at a suitably high level should deal with these issues by meeting with the parties in question, seeking consensus on the issues, or motivating the parties to achieve consensus during the workshop.

Teams often require a period of incubation in order to become comfortable and work well together. If adequate preparation time is not provided and/or if a briefing meeting was not conducted, workshop progress may be slow the first day or so. Some teams will require a team building exercise to get them together. (For sample exercises of facilitation techniques refer to Odell [Martin, 1996].)

Some tips for user workshops include the following

- Based on their expertise, various participants may provide temporary leadership or team-up with the facilitator. Use sparingly when practical.
- Project managers and executive sponsors should not be facilitators for user workshops in which they have a stake in the outcome. Unbiased facilitation and impartiality will be compromised.
- To improve clarity, avoid technical jargon.
- Plan for anticipated cultural changes.

Acknowledgment

This article contains significant portions of the OO methodology developed by James Martin and Co. The author would like to thank them for their kind contribution.

REFERENCES

Martin, James, and James J. Odell, *Object-Oriented Methods: Pragmatic Considerations,* Prentice-Hall, Englewood Cliffs, NJ, 1996.

Object-Oriented Methodologies

January 1996

OO AND METHODOLOGY

One of the primary differences between traditional and OO methodologies is that traditional approaches were limited to developing conventional data-processing systems. On the other hand, OO methodologies can be used to develop *any* kind of system—whether or not the system is implemented using OO technology.

For many years, object orientation has been associated exclusively with a particular kind of programming language. Today, the notions employed by OO programming languages (OOPLS) are applied as a general philosophy for system development. This does not mean that OO systems development is specified in terms of classes that physically encompass definitions of object variables and coded methods. Nor does this mean that a system is specified in terms of inherited code. While the notions of class structures and inheritance are used to define object orientation, they are in fact just *implementations* of OO. Conceptually, object orientation has come to be interpreted more generally.

Primarily, this broader interpretation means that OO is a way of organizing our thoughts about our world. This organization is based on the types of things—or *object types*—in our world. In this way, we can define the attributes of these object types, operations performed on these object types, rules based on them, machine learning on them, and so on. Instead of one physical unit that contains variables and methods, a more general OO approach provides a way of organizing our knowledge conceptually. Object orientation, then, provides an index for our knowledge—whether that

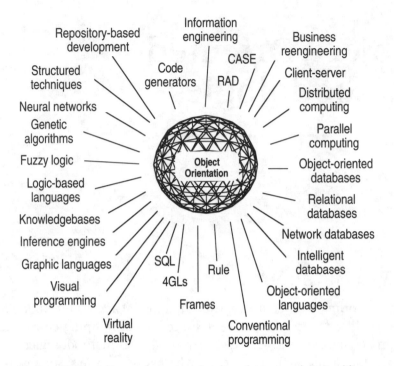

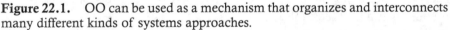

Figure 22.1. OO can be used as a mechanism that organizes and interconnects many different kinds of systems approaches.

knowledge is expressed in terms of rules, logic, functions, relational languages, neural networks, or something else. By extending this idea further, OO can be employed as an approach for organizing and interconnecting many different software technologies including knowledgebase, parallel computing, business reengineering, and rapid application development (Fig. 22.1).

OO is not Limited to Information Systems

In many organizations, application software development is performed by information systems (I.S.) personnel. While information is an important product of software systems, it is certainly not all that is involved. Systems for stock transfers, patient monitoring, and plant controls are not information systems. Their primary purpose is not the *information* they impart, but the *process* they perform. In fact, providing information is just another process like any other software process. Operations on a Stock object could include create, terminate, transfer, display_current_activity, or print_initial_offer_date. In other words, the OO systems developer is not limited to the world of information; she is free to specify any kind of process for automation. In addition, she can specify and program the system with a number of approaches (e.g., rules, functions, logic, SQL). Perhaps a more descriptive name for this kind of person would be *software-application engineer.* The term *information system,* then, should be limited to only those processes that provide information.

This is not a diatribe on who should be called what, but rather on who should be *doing* what. The point above stresses that software system developers are not exclusively in the business of providing information or even processing data. Their business is developing and implementing software solutions for the organization. Today, the best technology available for organizing and interconnecting such development is object orientation. This means employing OO as a development philosophy—not just as a software language.

OO for Systems in General

In addition to going beyond just one kind of programming language, can the OO approach take us beyond software systems in general? Granted, software engineering is a specialty that will survive for many years to come. Software, however, is just one possible mechanism for system implementation. Particularly in this era of business-process reengineering (BPR), the emphasis is on *any* business process—not just those automated by software.

The question is whether an OO approach can be effectively used for business systems in general. Can OO be used to understand and specify non-software-related—as well as software-related—processes? The answer, of course, is yes. In fact, OO was born from the need for an easier way to simulate systems—not just simulation of information systems but *any* kind of system. The founding fathers of Simula determined that managing one big process was not the answer. Rather, the solution consisted of many components that interacted with one another. These components were not based on some ad hoc modularization. Instead, they were based on the types, or classes, of things being simulated. The structure and behavior of the system, then, could easily be located and manipulated.

While Simula developed into the first object-oriented programming language, its most important legacy was a philosophical one. Object orientation provides a way for engineering any kind of system—regardless of how the system will be implemented. In addition, this same object-oriented engineering specification can be used to guide many other disciples, whether they involve people, machines, or computers (Fig. 22.2).

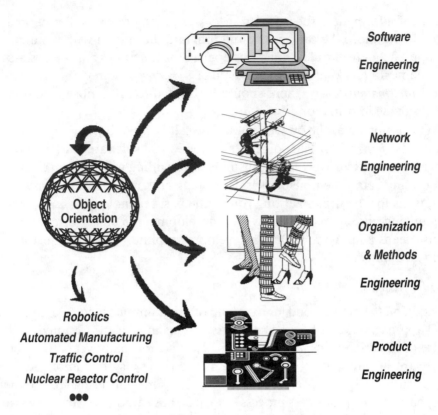

Figure 22.2.   Object orientation can support disciplines.

OO METHODOLOGY PHASES

System-development methodologies address some or all of the following system-development life cycle (SDLC) phases: planning, analysis, design, construction, and transition. The exact phases are not defined by the gods and etched onto tablets. However, they are phases that must be addressed in some manner if an organization is to support *full lifecycle* system development. Whatever you want to call them and however you want to group them, OO methodologies must still address these SDLC phases.

Strategy Planning

> Strategy planning produces high-level models of a business and, with them, defines a plan to develop a set of interrelated system projects.

Strategy planning takes a wide view of the business needs and direction to ensure that short term decisions fit with long term aims. The scope may be an area identified in the business plan. It may be an organizational or functional grouping. It may be identified as a value stream resulting from business reengineering. It may even be the enterprise as a whole. The common characteristic is the need to build compatible, consistent, and—one hopes—automatable support for the business.

The strategy plan defines a set of interrelated system projects, and it provides a basic description and delivery schedule for each project. The strategy plan does not include a plan for *every* individual project in the future. Instead, it is a high-level map within which detailed projects will be planned at more tactical and operational levels. The map ensures that small, iterative projects can be reassembled into cooperating, enterprise systems.

System Analysis

> System analysis models a system area based on the domain expert's concepts—deferring any decisions related to implementation.

System analysis is regarded as the first phase of most system projects. It focuses on understanding the business in terms of its activities, rules, locations, and information. When reengineering a business, the analysis *goes* beyond just looking at information to include *anything* or *anybody* of interest to the business.

The problem with many traditional analysis methods is that they emphasize a complete, detailed, and exhaustive approach which is, at best, impractical and, in many cases, impossible. This emphasis on detail gives rise to analysis paralysis. Lengthy analysis projects are incompatible with the goals of system development. The objectives of system analysis are to understand the business so that the systems will support the business, to scope and prioritize the system-design areas, and to establish a basis for iterative development.

The analysis identifies object types, event types, and business rules, and it employs usage analysis techniques. These are crucial for the correct development of automated—as well as nonautomated—systems. Using objects and events provides a model of the business that is closer to how we humans understand the world. Hence, it gives a basis for a design based on real world concepts. Business rules and usage document the business practice in a way that preserves flexibility for distribution decisions in design.

System Design

> System design develops an implementation model
> based on the conceptual models developed during
> system analysis.

System design is not an "extension" to system analysis. It takes the conceptual models developed during system analysis and maps them into implementation models. It involves designing the look and feel of the application and making the technical design decisions—including deciding on data and process distribution. Performance and resource requirements are important considerations here. Usability, however, is key to a successful application.

For many systems, the design stage is driven by user interface design. As such, this stage should maximize consistency and reusability in the designs. Here, the design approach should use a process of visualizing the user tasks, abstracting to identify common and similar components, and detailing the interface through prototyping. For client/server systems, the major decisions in design concern distributing process and data.

Before finalizing a system design, the stability and robustness of the design are evaluated and enhanced where needed.

System Construction

> System construction involves building and testing
> programs, databases, and networks as defined during
> system design.

The act of construction does not change dramatically for client/server. One of the principle differences is that software is built in smaller pieces on multiple platforms. The recommended approach to client/server development begins with creating a simpler version of the environment for development purposes. For example, code is developed and tested against a workstation-resident database. Then, the application migrates to the true server environment. For client/server systems, unit and integration tasks are both part of constructing code. Systems and acceptance tests are both part of verifying the system operation. This kind of subtle change to the construction task greatly simplifies the task of building client/server applications.

System Transition

> System transition installs the constructed systems.

In systems development, the job is not over until the system is up and running in the user environment. System transition is concerned with getting the system into production—the last stage in development. In client/server development, increased attention should be given to establishing support services, software distribution, and continuous training.

System Maintenance

System maintenance is an additional phase that many developers address as part of the system lifecycle. In this phase, the system is enhanced to include such deliverables as bug fixes, performance and usability improvements, and general realignment with business practices. Such enhancements are not usually considered as part of the same development project as the original system development. Typically, such enhancements are scheduled as yet another system-development project that can also include analysis, design, construction, and transition phases. Maintenance, then, becomes a SDLC project—and is scheduled just like any other project. Such scheduling can be defined during the construction phase of the original project or during the planning phase. In this way, system maintenance does not require a separate phase, *per se*. Instead, it can be addressed during the planning through transition phases described above.

TWO MAJOR GOALS

The methodology described above employs an object-oriented approach to thinking about a system. It does not, however, require an OO implementation. An OO way of thinking can be used to develop *any* kind of system—whether or not the system is implemented using OO technology.

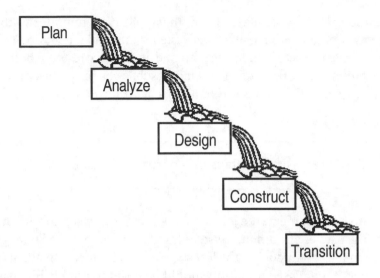

Figure 22.3. A *waterfall* approach to a full SDLC methodology.

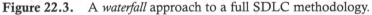

Promote Intentional Reuse

Reuse of analysis, design, and implementation components is a powerful facility. It leads to dramatic increases in productivity and quality while at the same time promoting consistency. Many of the tools available today provide object-oriented capabilities that facilitate reuse. However, the availability of such functionality does not in itself *require* reuse.

Reaping the rewards of reuse requires both an understanding of the possible future use of a component and a commitment to build the component for reuse. Building a truly reusable component takes more time and effort. The decision to invest in reuse must be part of the planning process. Any OO methodology must promote intentional reuse—rather than accidental reuse.

Lay the Foundation for Iterative Development

Many development projects employ a *waterfall* approach, illustrated in Fig. 22.3. Such an approach usually delivers too little, too late. While most methodologies can still be employed in a waterfall manner, a more iterative approach is recommended. This means picking the smallest, most meaningful aspect of the system and delivering the benefit to the business as early as possible. Then, iterate and deliver some more. Each iteration can contain components that may be developed concurrently by coordinating multiple—yet interrelated—projects. Here, it is possible to employ a spiral approach, as illustrated in Fig. 22.4.

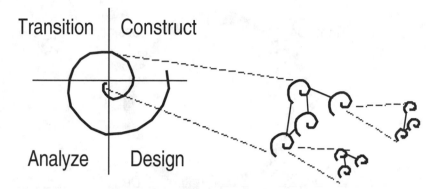

Figure 22.4. A *spiral* approach to development methodology that employs concurrent system development.

CONCURRENT ENGINEERING AND THE SDLC

In terms of SDLC, concurrent engineering (CE) is a systematic approach to the integrated, concurrent development of automated systems. First, this means that CE involves making the various components of a system interoperable. For instance, Fig. 22.4 illustrates that a single development spiral can be implemented instead as multiple spirals. In order for these components to communicate within a system, the project teams must also communicate. In a CE environment, direct communication between projects is important. However, if too much communication causes project delays, the number of interrelated projects must be reduced. In CE, each spiral is expected to be a component in its own right, yet is not developed in its own vacuum.

Another aspect of CE is that it applies *within* each project. In the waterfall and spiral approaches, each phase lays the foundation for the next phase. So, it is important to proceed methodically. In CE, however, these phases can overlap, so that much of the work within a project can proceed concurrently. For example, Fig. 22.5 illustrates the way in which a

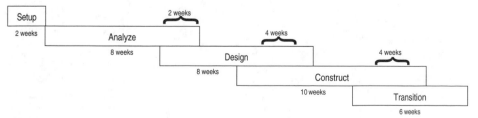

Figure 22.5. A *mini-waterfall* approach using concurrent engineering and a timebox of 120 days.

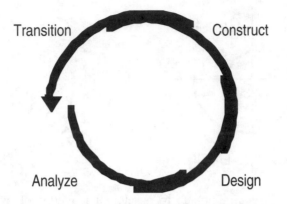

Transition   Construct

Analyze   Design

Figure 22.6.   Concurrent engineering employed within a spiral.

waterfall approach can be adapted to CE. In this particular example, the development time was limited, or *timeboxed,* to be completed in 120 days. Furthermore, this one concurrent waterfall could be one *mini-waterfall* component of a much larger waterfall similar to that depicted in Fig. 22.3.

If a spiral approach to system development is preferred, Fig. 22.6 illustrates how concurrent engineering can be applied to each iteration of a spiral. Furthermore, spirals with overlapping phases can be employed along with the concurrent spiral approach depicted on the right of Fig. 22.4.

REFERENCE

Carter, Donald E., and Barbara Stilwell Baker, *Concurrent Engineering: The Product Development Environment of the 1990s,* Addison-Wesley, Reading, MA, 1992.

Index

Page references followed by italic *n* refer to material in footnotes.